"*The most important ingredi.*
spirit of the person standing _
*mixes an inspiring story of how caring for others is not only a
great business model but a proven path for professional growth that
creates meaningful relationships on both sides of the bar. I admire
how lovingly* Pouring With Heart *inspires those around them to
mix into each drink a memorable appreciation for humanity.*"
–Danny Meyer, author, *Setting the Table,*
The Transforming Power of Hospitality in Business

"*Cedd Moses and his team know the bar business as well as anyone
on the planet. Read* Pouring with Heart *if you want to learn the
secret to their amazing success.*"
–Caroline Rosen, former President, Tales of the Cocktail;
global leader in spirits and cocktail education

"*If you want to be successful in the bar business, there is no better
authority than Cedd Moses. He has created amazing bars, and his
calling is building careers for bartenders.*"
–Jack McGarry, Managing Partner, The Dead Rabbit;
author; winner of the World's Best Bar award

"*Cedd Moses has dedicated his life to the bar business and building the careers of many bartenders. Now, he is spreading this dedication to thousands more in the bar business with this book. It is his calling in life, and now more than ever, our industry needs some help in rebuilding.*"
—Ivy Mix, author, *Spirits of Latin America: A Celebration of Culture & Cocktails*

"*I'm only here today because a boss like Cedd Moses invested in me like I was a future businessman while I was washing dishes at a truck stop. To know Cedd is changing the lives of thousands at his venues around the country gives me hope for the next generation of hospitality leaders.*"
—Sean Finter, Founder, Barmetrix; coach; speaker

"*Cedd is not only a visionary, a disruptive entrepreneur, and a remarkable human being but a true heart-led leader unlike anyone I've ever met in the bar business. This industry is not for the faint of heart, but if you are looking for someone to help you on your way toward a fulfilling career, I can't think of a better guide than Cedd on this earth.*"
—Daniel del Olmo, President, Sage Hospitality Management

"*Cedd Moses is dedicated to building thousands of careers in the bar business. Not jobs. Careers. It is his calling in life, and it's so needed in these challenging times for the hospitality industry.*"
—Brent Rosen, President and CEO, National Food and Beverage Foundation

POURING WITH HEART

POURING

WITH HEART

THE ESSENTIAL MAGIC
BEHIND THE BARTENDERS
WE LOVE

CEDD MOSES
ERIK CARDONA

LIONCREST
PUBLISHING

Registration #34234390

Hardcover ISBN: 978-1-5445-2528-0
Paperback ISBN: 978-1-5445-2526-6
eBook ISBN: 978-1-5445-2527-3
Audiobook ISBN: 978-1-5445-2529-7

DEDICATION

I've been in love with the bar world for a long time.

I never thought I'd see the day it could all be taken away. When you're in love, you seldom stop to think about what your life might be without it. COVID-19 painted us a grim picture. The pandemic threatened our industry in a way that most of us caught in its wake will never recover from. Those of us who were fortunate to make it through have scars. Those who did not make it through, *we remember in our hearts.*

Like many of us out there, the pandemic changed me. I took it personally. Watching storied locations close down. Some bars I frequented. Some bars I had on my wish list to saddle up to. But more difficult to bear was waking each morning to seemingly worse news coming from every corner of the planet. Millions being laid off. Overnight. Wondering if bar culture as we knew it would ever be the same. And then, gravely, if we might lose our bars for good.

And then a funny thing happened. *Despite being shut down first and called nonessential. Despite being scorned as super spreaders. Despite shouldering an unfair blame for contributing to the onset of the pandemic—determined, defiant teams behind the bar didn't quit. They went to work. They kept serving and being of service to their community. They dug as deep as humanly possible to keep our profession alive during the scariest time of our generation. Of a century's worth of generations.* Those people. Our people. Our bar families went to work. *Trying, throughout, not to let their fear and anxiety show. Not to let on the overwhelming emotion that came with the sudden financially precarious spots they landed in.* Most went without the money for basic essentials. Food to fill their refrigerators. Rent to keep the roof over their heads. Many of whom were living without health insurance to fall back on. Insecure about their own chances of survival should they come into contact with the virus. *Or worse, whether they'd contract it, become a silent host, and live with the remorse of killing their grandparents. But still, they didn't cave.* They stared that son of a bitch in its cold, black, pandemic fucking heart. And in doing so, opted to pour with theirs. They went to work. Missing their regulars that could no longer sit at their bar. Longing for connection. Interaction. The back slaps, the toasts, the hugs, the high-fives. The handshake. All things of the past. Still, these bar teams remained stalwart professionals. They went to work. Incessantly cleaning and disinfecting after each and every customer. Wearing enough gear to disarm a bomb. Masks. Double masks. Face shields. Throwaway garments. Glasses. Gloves. They went to work. With fear in their eyes and sweat through their shirts. *They were scared. You could see it in their mannerisms. You could hear it in their voice.* Yet still, a brave face. A sign of confidence to the community *that their local bar could be a safe place. A place to celebrate life in spite of a nightmare situation. They stayed strong so that the customer, who was also afraid, could feel like there was something in their life that was okay. They went to work.* Supporting their community when their community needed them most. Refusing to cut bait, tapping *into their last ounce of courage and strength for us. Opening their doors for us, while their house was seemingly falling apart around them. They went to work in the worst hour. And because they did, it became their finest hour. To* the bar teams of 2020 *that* kept the flame burning for our industry.

I proudly dedicate this book to you all.

"In the past, jobs were about muscles, now they're about brains, but in the future, they'll be about the heart."

–Dame Minouche Shafik, London School of Economics

CONTENTS

FOREWORD

by Dale DeGroff

T he proposition:

We go to bartenders, <u>not</u> to bars.

When I arrived in New York City in 1969, I stepped off the train with a backpack and a guitar and no return ticket. I hit a wall of heat and humidity on 34th Street as I left the station; luckily, it was a short walk to my lodging, the Sloan House YMCA. I had visited NYC on weekends, but it was a much different feeling knowing that I was going to *live* in the middle of Manhattan; it seemed much bigger all of a sudden. I was seeing the city through different eyes, and I wanted to find out what was going on behind all those windows.

I left university at the end of my junior year with an extremely finite cash reserve, confident that I'd be on Broadway in no time. And I was exactly right: to this day, at no time have I ever set foot on a Broadway stage. But eventually, I became familiar with a different set of floorboards: the wooden-slatted ones designed to protect a bartender's back while pulling ten- to twelve-hour shifts.

The first time I walked into Paddy McGlade's bar a couple weeks later in 1969, I was still carrying my backpack and my guitar. I couldn't leave anything in my room at the YMCA; the chance that my belongings would still be there when I returned was rated by the desk clerk at less than 40 percent. Those were odds I couldn't afford, so I needed a new place to live. Which is why I walked into Paddy McGlade's that night.

My hair was long, and when I darkened the door of McGlade's, every head swiveled and all eyes locked on me. Everyone looked at me like a side dish they hadn't ordered. Everyone, *except* the elderly gentleman behind the bar, who greeted me as I approached with a friendly "What'll it be, young man?" A short, dour-looking man sitting in the corner of the bar was not happy to see me, and he expressed his unhappiness with a grunt. Eventually, I heard the name "Paddy" repeated a few times and realized that they were referring to him, the owner. But his unhappiness seemed to have no effect on the bartender's cheerful demeanor. There was, however, a noticeable change in the demeanor of the rest of the old dudes around the bar when they saw that Al, the bartender, was okay with me.

I sang Hank Williams's "Your Cheatin' Heart" three times that night and got a free beer each time I did! The apartment didn't pan out, but when I moved to the neighborhood in 1970, McGlade's became my bar. I found out the source of Paddy's unhappiness. He sent money home to his family, who were members of the IRA. He kept his friends close around him day and night. It was private and serious business Paddy was involved in, and there was little room for joy in his life.

But McGlade's was a joyous place. Al kept it full with an interesting cross section of humanity. It took three years of regular attendance before Paddy bought me a drink, of course. Al extended that courtesy much earlier in my tenure. When Al was behind the bar, he was the boss, and even though Paddy owned the place and sat in the corner of the bar day and night, when Al made a call, it was final. Paddy would never think of overruling him.

We go to bartenders, <u>not</u> to bars.

New York had three thousand bars the year I arrived. They were our natural resource like the redwoods in California, and a good bartender was like a forest ranger, happy to guide you and quick to sort out danger or trouble. The New York City bar, going back to the early nineteenth century, was the benchmark against which all bars were measured. In the late nineteenth to early twentieth century, when business became a global affair and Americans traveled abroad in large numbers, we began exporting the American bar. Major hotels in Paris, Rome, and London had an "American bar." Prohibition in the United States added to that tally, as many top bartenders were drawn to Europe. Prohibition decimated the profession on this side of the Atlantic, and it would take decades to recover.

The hit that the culinary side of bars took in the first half of the twentieth century from wars and economic disaster brought us processed and convenience foods sold in giant supermarkets, and the bar business did not escape unscathed. After Prohibition, shortcuts to solve the problem of unskilled labor diminished the quality of the classic drinks of the golden age of the cocktail. Artificial sour mixes took the place of fresh ingredients, and many spirits used in cocktails simply disappeared after Prohibition. But even though bartending was still considered a gangster profession in the years after Prohibition, the gathering places where people pursued the art of living in a community of friends, the neighborhood bar, was still presided over by a welcoming presence, the bartender. The men, and the sadly few women, behind the bar in the late twentieth century still presided over, even curated, wonderful bars where life continued unabated. Bars were still gathering places that operated at a human pace, with the kind of human interaction that forms communities.

We go to bartenders, <u>not</u> to bars.

In the late twentieth century, bartending in the United States began a slow rehabilitation that would revive the profession as a proper career. Cedd Moses and the Pouring With Heart bar group have made it their calling to create careers in the bar business. I'm not talking about marginal work for poor students who don't fit into the world of college-educated professionals. I am referring to a craft that requires a whole set of life skills. Both on the culinary side—the cocktail is America's first culinary art—and on the human side. The skills required are substantial: well-developed powers of observation, a deeper understanding of human nature, an innate need to reach out and help, and an ability to work together with a team of like-minded individuals who share the same qualities and the same vision. And of course, the skill to produce libations with a high degree of deliciousness, quickly, with style, and while holding three or four different conversations up and down the bar. They don't have a course for that in college; it is an old-school master/apprentice profession.

We go to bartenders, <u>not</u> to bars.

Andrew Abrahamson wasn't college material after graduating high school. He headed to Europe to live a little before moving on to whatever was next. In northern Spain, he walked into an Irish bar run by a mother-daughter duo, and after serving him his drink, the mother asked what nationality he was. Andrew is American, but he let her know that he's part Irish. That was good enough for her. He spent the summer behind the bar working for meals, all he could drink, and a room, but no pay. He had never worked in a bar before. Andrew was too young to tend bar when he returned to the United States, so he got a job as a barback in an Olive Garden in Seattle, waiting for the day he turned twenty-one and could get behind the bar again.

In 2007, Andrew read an article in the *Los Angeles Times* about Cedd Moses, an entrepreneurial maverick who was embarking on a singular mission: opening or restoring dive bars in old buildings in forgotten neighborhoods in Downtown Los

Angeles. The article featured the third bar that Cedd's group opened, called Seven Grand. Seven Grand was on the second floor of a handsome building at 515 West 7th Street, in the old financial district. The four-story building with a Spanish Colonial façade was built in 1921 and was the original home of Brock and Company Jewelry; it also housed the legendary Clifton's Silver Spoon Cafeteria. Cedd loved old downtown architecture, but he loved even more the dive bars that dotted the downtown neighborhoods. He had already rescued a failing saloon dating from pre-Prohibition on West 8th Street, the Golden Gopher.

Andrew was swept away by the article. He wanted a gig at Seven Grand so badly, he applied over and over again until, one night, he sat down and wrote an impassioned email to Cedd's GM at the time, David Fleisher, who responded with an offer to barback. Andrew took it on the spot. Cedd recognized Andrew immediately as a perfect fit for leadership within the company. One of Cedd's strongest attributes, an uncanny ability to hire the right people, has been key to the success of Pouring With Heart. Seven years later, in 2014, Andrew was promoted to director of the three spirits bars in the company: the whiskey bar Seven Grand; Caña Rum Bar; and the home of agave spirits, Las Perlas. In 2019, Andrew was appointed chief operations officer for twenty-five bars across four states, a new position in the company.

How does that happen? And how does a company go from zero to twenty-five bars in eighteen years? There are lots of answers for both of those questions, but at the heart of it, there are two reasons, and they also explain why Cedd embarked on growth for the company in the first place.

Andrew enlightened me when he remarked in our interview, "I never met an owner who loved bars more than Cedd! He would dress up to come to Seven Grand, wearing a top hat and carrying a cane. Cedd loved to host groups and show off the joint."

Cedd would have a different answer. He spent years in the bars in Los Angeles, all through the days he worked in finance, and frankly expressed that he was at his happiest in dive bars with the bartenders, the barbacks, and the regulars. His change of life to become a hospitality professional saved him from "spiritual bankruptcy." He found his calling in creating careers for the people he related to most.

For nine thousand years, since the hunter-gatherers, the skill to sustain the life of the tribe with food and drink has been a noble and worthwhile endeavor. The tribe at Cedd's bar group, Pouring With Heart, consists of nearly four hundred souls, all working with a common goal and all working with a family of people they love and are proud to work alongside. Pouring With Heart is not your average bar group! Most of the people came to the company with limited opportunities. Most started in entry-level service positions and built successful careers, and this bar group has become their life and family. And that's why building careers has so much personal meaning to Cedd.

Cedd Moses grew up in the post-disco, punk scene of Hollywood in the early 1980s, and he is no stranger to the Los Angeles nightlife scene. He played in a punk band, so he spent time in the clubs and the underground music scene. We are all grateful that Cedd fell in love with bars with *surroundings of substance* and that they became his passion.

In 2009, Cedd offered to partner in the back room at Cole's French Dip restaurant with Eric Alperin, the author of *Unvarnished* and the director of education at Pouring With Heart, and Sasha Petraske, a New York bar owner whose Milk & Honey bar inspired a generation of bartenders around the world. Eric and Sasha were looking for an expansion property in Los Angeles. Their craft cocktail bar, The Varnish, opened in that space later in 2009. The Varnish and Cedd's Seven Grand put Los Angeles back into the heart of the craft bar movement. Sasha, like Cedd, loved bars, and he surrounded himself with like-minded people.

Success for Cedd and Pouring With Heart has never been defined solely by net gain or a positive bottom line. For them, the profits made are the fuel for more careers. Money coming in the door, at any rate, becomes meaningless if the culture of the company is sick and employees don't thrive and succeed as the company succeeds. This book is an extension of their philosophy in proving that bartending can be a successful career.

Let's raise a glass in cheers to Pouring With Heart.

INTRODUCTION

"When you drank the world was still out there,
but for the moment it didn't have you by the throat."
—Charles Bukowski, *Barfly* writer and poet

Stench.

The nose-burning smell of bacteria fermenting with black mold, if I had to guess. The kind of vile you'd expect at a coroner's office.

Or a crime scene.

Only we hadn't crossed any police tape. We'd just asked the bartender which way to the john.

You could taste the dank seeping through the corridor walls, replacing the oxygen and filling our lungs with its reek—one uninvited waft after another—the farther we made it down the hall.

Enough to make your nose turn. Your eyes burn.

And it only got worse when we entered what I can only describe as the dirtiest bathroom I'd ever witnessed outside of a developing country. We were in a glorified open sewer.

Inside, strung out somewhere between the feces stains and broken mirrors that cluttered the floor, was the bar manager. We were supposed to meet that night, but part of me began to think we'd fallen off his calendar, considering he was crouched in the corner smoking a crack pipe.

It was the spring of 2001. And we were at the storied Golden Gopher bar in Downtown LA.

A bar that was hardly recognizable from when I was there a decade prior.

The bar manager, high as a kite, hardly noticed us. Nor did the rest of the seemingly desperate clientele inside.

In the bathroom, exposed wiring and plumbing peeked out from the stucco walls that had been kicked in. The rusted pipes were stained brown from years of discharge. You didn't know where the pipes were going, but you knew the brown fluid running out of them was coming with it.

I took my leak in record time, making sure to keep one hand over my mouth so as not to add to the puke already inside the urinal walls. I needed a drink.

A *stiff* drink.

We made our way to a torn-apart bar top. Not haggard or unkept. More like disemboweled. Saddling up, you couldn't help but feel bad for this once historic watering hole. Whether it's a pub, tavern, alehouse, or saloon, bars have their own soul. And this one was suffering.

It wasn't just poorly run. This bar was abused.

And like a wounded animal that's accepted its fate, I could feel it begging for mercy from my barstool. To show it the kindness of putting a bullet in it before going on my way.

"What the fuck do you want?" the bartender cursed in our direction.

His eyes were swollen, doing their best to shy away from human contact while we picked between the only two bottles of booze in the joint. Gin…and gin. Both bottles were warm and occupied by an equally disconcerting amount of flies buzzing around their stoppers.

There were no tools or tins. No fruit or garnishes to be found. The well wasn't exactly set up for service. It was set up for selling cigarettes and bottles in paper bags out the back door.

And crack.

Instead of drugs, we ordered two gin and tonics. Except he didn't have tonic, so gin and sodas were what we got.

No ice.

Nothing like a gin and soda, neat, to warm the cockles.

The high-as-fuck bartender demanded we pay up front, and when we did, he put *our* money in *his* wallet.

What the fuck was going on with this place?

As we would discover later, the Gopher was over a year behind on rent. It had been overrun by the local 18th Street gang, the most dangerous in town. Their deed was signed in spray paint throughout the foreboding, albeit colorful, gang markings that wallpapered the interior. In truth, the Golden Gopher wasn't so much a bar business as it was a front for drug dealing and prostitution.

The same stomping grounds the twenty-sixth president of the United States, Teddy Roosevelt, made famous for his patronage in 1905. He rode into the Gopher on horseback, for fuck's sake.

Imagine if Teddy could see, past his mustache and monocle, what I was witnessing in front of me almost a full century later.

The decision to buy that rat-infested shithole would define the future direction of my life, along with the lives of hundreds more that have since joined our bar group.

Or as we like to call it, our bar family.

THIS BOOK IS FOR YOU

Maybe you're reading this book because you feel marginalized by Corporate America. Welcome to the club. A lot of us don't belong in a traditional nine to five. And when you find yourself outside of the fishbowl, the work opportunities available to you, or lack thereof, can be disheartening.

I tried to fit in the fishbowl, and I can tell you firsthand, for me, it felt soulless and empty. No one really gave a shit about each other in any of the offices I ever worked in. And most of my colleagues spent their workdays counting down the minutes until quitting time so they could go home (or to a bar).

Maybe you're looking for something different. You've heard about bars and bartending, but you want to know what *really* makes them tick. What makes them thrive. What makes a bar family come to work and feel alive.

Or maybe you're already working behind a bar, but you're struggling to achieve your goals there.

Whatever the case, you picked up the right book. I know you did because I wrote it for you. I wrote it for all of us out there who know the feeling of feeling like we don't belong.

PROMISES, PROMISES

If you're not working behind a bar yet, this book will shed light on why the bar business is ripe with opportunities for you to succeed. It will also share with you the step-by-step secrets to achieving that success. The kind of success careers are made of. Yes, I just said "career" when referring to bartending.

Confidently.

Most of the employees who make up our bar family, college degrees or not, earn the hourly wages typically reserved for those with PhDs. I promise to let you in on all kinds of other truths about working behind the bar and, more importantly, how to free yourself of some of the myths out there that might be holding you back.

And here's my second promise to you: if you're someone who wants to bring passion and enthusiasm to our industry, I won't just teach you how to get in the door.

I'll teach you how to knock it down.

Yes, you can make a career out of this. And you can make a damn good living in the process. Enough for a family. A home. A nice car and, eventually, if it's in the cards, college tuition for your kids.

Not only that, but you'll learn there's nobility in being of service to others. You'll learn how much pride comes with the job and why people—dating back to the origins of this country—have, in turn, treated bartenders with the utmost respect.

The torch was lit long before you. The question is, do you have what it takes to carry it? To provide a safe and memorable place for people to come and, as Bukowski said, free themselves of the world's grip around their throat?

DON'T WORRY—I'M NOT FULL OF SHIT (ANYMORE)

I struggled to find my career until I finally found my true purpose in life. Nothing has given me more satisfaction than working alongside my fellow bar family, cultivating careers for people who, like me, have felt like outsiders everywhere else.

"Outsiders" are my fucking people.

I felt like an outsider until I discovered the bar business. But now I'm surrounded by the most wonderful people every day, and I'm grateful. I'm grateful to work with people fueled by passion and pride for their craft. Who put themselves in a position of service to others and not the other way around.

Some people call them "the help." To me, those are fighting words.

And frankly, it's ignorant considering this country was founded on all of us being "the help." It's the can-do spirit. The get-the-job-done mentality. The *you-before-me* tenet of the service industry that's responsible for more than just building successful bars. It builds character. It builds communities. And it built this country.

From time to time in this book, I'll debunk a few of the clichéd myths I've come across in my twenty-five years in this business.

It's important that I share with you why these myths are bullshit. However, more specifically, in this book you will learn:

- What it means to Pour with Heart

- Why Pouring with Heart works, and how it's the magic behind a bartender's success

- How to get a bar job and turn that bar job into a great career

- How to find the right bar for you (and avoid the one that will sink your career before it starts)

- How to bring customers back, and the value they offer you when you're working behind the bar

- The importance of being a great barback

- Strategies on how to move from barbacking to bartending to leading your own bar

- The pitfalls to avoid when working at a bar—the seductions, temptations, and traps that can derail your career (or worse)

- How to become an absolute legend behind the bar

What you'll read here about bartending will surprise you. Mostly because it flies in the face of conventional wisdom.

Believe it or not, I'll use math, science, and especially history—tons of data you'd never think would be relative to a discussion about booze and bartenders—to support the findings in this book. I'll lay it all out for you.

Trust me: regardless of what you look like, where you've been, or what you've failed at in the past, there's a place for you here alongside us.

I'm no stranger to failure. I was a money-managing Wall Street hotshot with his face on the cover of *Forbes* by the time I was thirty. And I was miserable. The temptations that come with wealth and power did their best to numb me from my emptiness. But when your soul isn't right, your body and mind don't stand a chance.

Every room, every office, every meeting felt claustrophobic. Despite the thousand monitors keeping track of stocks around the world. Eighteen floors up, confined in a hermetically sealed, Class-A office building that felt more sterile than the ICU at Johns Hopkins. The only language we spoke started and ended with the word "profit." How much money could we make off the mistakes of less sophisticated investors? We had an edge born from long hours and short-term thinking that we fused into short-term gains.

But that was *all* we had.

That and the inescapable feeling that, as a human, I was slowly dying.

So despite an onslaught of criticism, I left the boardroom and never looked back. At the time, I didn't know what the cure for me would be, but I knew I sorely needed human connection. And I had an idea where I could find it.

The place where people put their arms around each other. Opened their hearts. Shared war stories, love stories, fistfights, teardrops, and second chances. Where they went for support when their chips were down. And to celebrate those precious moments when they weren't. Where their differences, *before* their similarities, made for interesting conversation. The place they went to sing. To laugh. To be honest…

To be human.

If I wanted to be among my people, I needed to get to my local bar.

But like I said before, I know failure. I fail all the fucking time. I'm probably failing right now as I write this book.

Walking into this business may have forever changed my life for the better. But make no mistake, I struggled for over a decade to figure out the proper way to run bars. It took years until my bar family and I landed on the magic that has led us to becoming one of the greatest bar success stories in modern American history.

And now, over the next nine chapters, I'm going to share that magic with you.

Note: I am not some genius.

I'm no smarter than the next person; plus, I'm *more* than a little bit crazy.

At least, that's what everyone said when I gave up my job in finance and bet my life savings on opening ten bars on Skid Row. Then they *really* thought I was crazy when our bar group doubled down and opened a dozen more bars in ghost towns across Texas, Colorado, and California.

Today, our bar family's mission is to create 2,030 careers in the bar business by the year 2030, which means opening another one hundred bars in the next decade.

Creating careers behind the bar is my life's purpose.

My father devoted his life to being an artist. He always told me that he would go crazy if he couldn't paint. He painted almost every day for sixty-five years and became famous doing it. But most importantly, he found his calling in life. The thing that gave him the most fulfillment and happiness. He painted until his body gave out at almost ninety-one years old, and then he passed away within a week.

I'm proud of my father's lifelong pursuit of what brought him the greatest fulfillment. And I'm so glad he passed that passion on to me to pursue my dreams as well.

This book is an expression of my calling in life. It's the best way I know how to share my experiences and make my knowledge *yours*.

Our bar family has helped start careers for more than four hundred young people, many of whom never thought they had a shot at success.

My kinda people.

You'll get to hear from several of them in this book. Most of whom have no college degree. Some were even homeless. Living on the fringes of society, where opportunity feels like a fairytale at best.

But all of them struggled to find a job they believed in. To work with, *and for,* people who believed in them too.

A good portion have earned a stake in our future growth across the country. They've built successful careers with us, and it makes me so damn proud. In doing so, they've helped me fulfill what I was put on this earth to do. And for that, I'll be forever indebted.

Now, it's your turn to forge your own path.

There's no reason you can't build a successful career like these folks in the best damn business on the planet.

POURING WITH HEART:
THE MAGIC BEHIND OUR SUCCESS

Conventional wisdom suggests that being successful at a bar means bartending at the trendy new hot spot. That's false. We've been nationally ranked, Yelped about, tweeted about, blogged about, and bragged about. In some instances, labeled the *hottest* place in town by expert reviewers and aficionado magazines. Many of our bars have won awards for their drinks, design, and decor.

None of that equates to the true success of the bar or the bartenders working there.

Sure, some flare and publicity will bring people in, temporarily. But that stuff lacks the reason inherent in human nature that keeps people coming back over time. It lacks the magic that drives a diverse group of people to call that bar their home.

In this book, I'll show you that the real magic of bartending comes from Pouring with Heart. It's not just an idea; it's a philosophy. It's our mantra, our blood, our DNA.

Much like that of Mom's home cooking.

Mom's cooking isn't the best because she's the hippest mom in town. The reason nothing tastes better than her food is because it's made with love and served from the heart.

BARS HUMANIZE US

Bars are special places for misfits like us.

I became obsessed with them by the time I could legally drink. Bars became my vehicle for connecting with the city in a real way. Where I finally felt comfortable opening up to total strangers. They're the place where I felt, and continue to feel, most at home.

Bars just might be the last refuge for humanity (and, specifically, your community) to come together without judgment. Free from the canned bullshit and stale environment of modern city living.

Modern city living…a true ratfuck.

Chockfull of corporate coffee houses misrepresenting themselves as the "Third Place." Championing themselves as equitable, diverse, and inclusive cultures where communities are welcome to come and gather freely between home and work. But a closer look at these corporate chains reveals an empty promise. A blatant bait-and-switch with one goal in mind. Manipulation. Something bad for the human spirit but great for businesses that prefer to cattle-call sheep by the masses, shear them, and make off with the spoils. These business chains don't inspire thinking or conversation. Their very blueprints are born of efficiency charts and customer flow schematics designed to push people in and out with the least amount of human interaction possible. They prefer their customers be in a hurry, with their heads down, buried in their smart devices. Which translates to zero sense of community or camaraderie. Meanwhile, your local bar is serving both in spades.

When you can't distinguish between customer service and automated responses from a computer, we've got a problem. That's not a shot at technology, but AI-driven assistants like Alexa and Siri will never be able to relate to us on a human level.

The less time we spend being human, the more lonely we feel as humans. The less we begin to trust *other* humans. And as for the idea of kindness, respect, and love for ourselves—and for other humans—well, that notion might as well go fuck itself.

But your local watering hole is different.

It's one of the last places out there where you truly are allowed off the leash. There's a sense of honesty we share across a bar top. From Steel Town to Tinseltown, and every bar in between, the one thing you can bet you'll find...is the truth.

I'm betting everything on saving local watering holes, and I want to bring you along for the ride. Namely because bars have truly fulfilled their promise as that necessary "Third Place" in my life. And have done the same for centuries for millions of others in this country.

But also because every puritan and buzzkill who has ever tried to deny the community of the magic that comes from bars and bartenders has always been met by a stiff line of defense. With that said, I'm more than happy to take the first night's watch.

I'm honored.

Because that magic is worth fighting for, dammit.

LET'S FIND THE MAGIC TOGETHER

By now, you've probably picked up on a lot of things we have in common. One thing we don't have in common is that I've probably done a hell of a lot more stupid shit in my life. But over time, I've emphasized to myself the importance of learning from my mistakes.

A few years back, I put a tattoo on my arm that says, "WELL, FUCK" to remind me to always fail forward. That means owning up to my fuckups and getting better because of them. We are all human, and we've all messed up.

In this book, I'll dole out lessons I've had to learn the painful way.

Not the hard way. *The painful way.*

It's taken me decades of trial and error to figure it out, and I'm dying to share the magic I've discovered.

Cheers to your future success!

CHAPTER ONE

POURING WITH HEART

"The more one lives for others, the greater their life.
The more one gives to others, the greater their abundance."
−Lao Tzu, ancient Chinese philosopher

T his bar is not a safe place.

My partner and I had passed escrow, received the keys, and even started holding development meetings inside what was now our Golden Gopher bar. We came in with all our ideas and dreams, which we thought could wash the bad taste out of this bar's mouth. But the one thought that began and finished every decision we made early on was:

This bar is not a safe place.

And therefore, we couldn't afford to make poor decisions. Not only from a financial perspective. But from a safety standpoint. There's added pressure walking into your office each day knowing one mistake could seal your fate before it begins. But beyond that, we felt an enormous sense of responsibility.

The previous tenants were criminals. The day we moved in, there were more crack pipes in the place than there were working faucets. Two stories up, there was an entire floor that moonlighted as a warehouse for selling smack. Ex-cons would get out of jail, break into the neighboring apartments, then climb to their respective rooftops and jump onto ours in order to try to claim the space above us.

Not to mention we were in the armpit of LA at a time when the city led the nation in two nefarious categories. Gun violence and murders. With the privatization of mental health clinics and the onslaught of crack cocaine, Skid Row and schizophrenia became major problems for Downtown Los Angeles. And since our bar hours, like most bar hours, began after sundown, if you weren't barricaded in, you got a good look at the city's devolution each night as the clock crawled on its hands and bloody knees to two a.m.

In other words, before we could succeed, we needed to survive.

We had to treat each night like it was a life-or-death situation because one lapse in judgment, one oversight, one brain fart could take us to that scary place. So we set up a system for working in teams. No one worked alone in a room. No one walked alone to their cars. No one even took the trash out without using the buddy system. And when you're forced to rely on each other to survive your shift each night, you become more than close. You become brothers and sisters.

You become *family*.

This is where the seeds of our success were planted. Looking after one another, at an almost instinctual level, keeping our hearts open and our eyes wide. Constant vigilance.

Adversity is a great teacher like that. One day at a fucking time.

As we grew closer as a team, the bar itself began to stir from its slumber. You could feel the plaque lifting from the Gopher's jowls the more plumbing we replaced, wiring we brought up to code, and walls we patched and painted. Nine months of reconstructive surgery later, we had to turn the lights on.

Full disclosure, I didn't know what the fuck I was doing. But instinctively, I knew what was *right*. And what's right usually resonates.

I remember clear as day discussions with so-called experts saying in order to make the Gopher successful, we'd have to bus people in from Hollywood.

But we didn't need to bus anybody in. We already had a community we belonged to. The people who worked in the largest fashion district in the country. The artists and creatives who called the Downtown studios and lofts their homes. These were the people we were building our bar for.

Not to mention, my personal aversion to the *Hollywood elite*.

Over my dead body were we going to sell watered-down vodka cranberries, charge eighteen bucks an apple martini, and send thousand-dollar bottles of Grey Goose to tables.

Our community would have called us sellouts, and they would have been right.

Had we resorted to slimy promoters and bottle service, we'd have been out of business in a week. No one would be safe coming to and from this bar if the only effort we put into it banked on the glitz and glamour of a one-hit-wonder, one-night-stand kind of place.

Our bar needed to be timeless. It needed to be soulful. We needed to bury the sketchy-as-fuck, dangerous vibe six-feet deep and start over from the ground up.

We needed to be a rock for our community. We needed them to know we were there for them. Because the Gopher wasn't the only part of that community that needed to heal. Needed to mend.

We were all in this *together*.

We knew what was going on outside our doors. What was happening above our very own roof. And we knew that if we weren't coming from the heart with our customers, they'd have no reason to look past the wrought-iron bars in their windows.

4

If our bar family and community didn't bond, then we didn't stand a chance. That meant taking security seriously. Walking our customers back to their apartments to make sure they were safe. Letting our guests know that we were grateful for them being there.

A funny thing started happening. As we began to support our community, believe in our community—slowly and surely, the way a beaten dog might hesitantly poke its nose back out of its cage—our community gathered the courage to trust us.

They showed up. And we never forgot that.

A community encumbered by the danger that surrounded it, that had *no* reason for stepping foot out of their homes.

We gave them one. And there's honor in that.

Like I said earlier, adversity is a hell of a teacher. If we didn't take care of each other and our community, we would have failed. And the consequences of that failure would have gone far past losing sales on a Friday night.

It's time we dive in head first with what it means to Pour with Heart. Because if I don't deliver on this concept, then the rest of this book doesn't mean a damn thing.

DO YOU BELIEVE IN MAGIC?

You don't open twenty-five bars in twenty years without a little luck. You don't keep those bars *open* without a little magic.

I've best heard "luck" described as the crossroads where "hard work meets opportunity." Luck, to me, has never strictly been a game of chance. If anything, it's the fortuitous bounce you get only *after* you've done everything in your power to put yourself in the right spot.

And just like luck, the word "magic" also has a little more depth to it.

The best bars you've ever been to. The best nights you've had out with friends. The best bartenders who made those nights special. If you think about the common thread between the memories that flood to mind, it's the magic.

That "something" in the air. The atmosphere. The electricity. The magic of relationships forming. Of strangers coming together, bonding over a common goal.

A common good.

In fact, the only thing you know better about the magic in a bar…is the absence of it.

You don't forget the stale, unwelcome vibe you bookmark in your mind when you close a tab knowing you'll never run a credit card in that establishment again.

For us, the *magic* you feel in a bar comes from the bartenders Pouring with Heart inside it.

We were lucky to discover this at the Golden Gopher. Early on, we were Pouring with Heart out of survival more than strategy. But in doing so, we were instilling a sense of trust in our community and a feeling of belonging with our customers. We were creating magic. And that magic was the reason those customers came back.

The fallacy of magic is that it can't be bottled. This book suggests otherwise.

Pouring with Heart is putting your heart and soul into being of service to the person right in front of you.

Now that you've opened the bottle, let's study the magic inside using data, science, and commonsense psychology to explore why Pouring with Heart works so damn well.

WHAT IT MEANS TO POUR WITH HEART

To better understand Pouring with Heart, we need to dig deeper than its surface-level definition. Pouring with Heart is a philosophy.

It's a credo. A belief system. An ideology.

It's an attitude.

More importantly, Pouring with Heart is a choice.

It's a decision you make prior to turning the lights on in your bar. Before the wells are stocked. The seats dusted off. And the jukebox plays its opening track.

Which means it's something everyone can do.

The catch is, no one can do it alone.

The service industry, in general, has an alarming percentage of bars and restaurants that go belly-up within the first twelve months of opening their doors.

I can spot the ones that will make it in the first twelve minutes of sitting at their bar.

It comes down to whether or not they're Pouring with Heart.

Most people think the objective of a bar is to pour drinks for customers, which you then charge money for, in exchange for some temporary real estate to sip said drinks. If you find yourself in that camp, please imagine my next line as though I were standing on a bar top, shouting into a megaphone framed by my two bare hands:

The bar business is not about drinks.

And it's not about how you make them. Obviously, every bar should aim for quality and presentation standards of excellence for the beer, wine, and cocktails being slung across it.

But what's *more* important to the success of a bar, to its longevity—to its ability to survive in the shark-infested waters that bars are routinely cast into with cinder blocks tied to their ankles—is that we don't mistake the act of *making* a drink with the art of *serving* one.

In fact, Pouring with Heart has nothing to do with "pouring" at all. It's not about technique, craftsmanship, or cocktail recipes.

Instead, Pouring with Heart is a guiding light. A metronome you can use to keep yourself, and your team, on track to succeed at what fuels the bar business:

Being of service.

This is our priority. Putting our heart and soul into doing just that. Being completely of service to those who entrust us with their patronage.

For some reason, proven by those bars still tied to their cinder blocks at the bottom of the service ocean, it's the easiest priority to lose track of.

Pouring with Heart helps keep that priority in focus.

When you lose that focus, your customers notice. They don't just see it. They experience it. They are part of that failure.

They *feel* it.

And it sticks with them.

> "The brain handles positive and negative information in different hemispheres. Negative emotions generally involve more thinking, and the information is processed more thoroughly than positive ones."
>
> **—Clifford Nass, Professor of Communication, Stanford University**

In short, one negative experience can wipe out several positive ones. Meaning, if you Pour with Heart ninety-nine times with someone who's a regular at your bar—but you're a jerk to them *once*—you could lose years of loyalty.

That's how strong the negativity bias is in human beings.

HOT SPOTS VS. HEART

I spent years focused on the wrong things. Chasing my tail trying to create the hippest bars in town. Measuring a given night's success by the amount of beautiful people we had wrapped around our building trying to get in. I was guilty of shallow, short-term thinking. Because the next week, the lines would stay the same length. Only, they would be wrapped around a different building. The same people, now waiting to get into a different hot spot that would inevitably open up down the street.

If a bar doesn't show loyalty to its customers, its customers sure as hell aren't going to show loyalty to that bar. To show loyalty, you can't rely on *providing* a service. You have to focus on *being* of service.

We've served our fair share of incredible cocktails and created trend-starting spirits programs. We've won a ton of awards and had exciting write-ups in major aficionado magazines. But plaques on the wall age like the rest of us. And though having an article written about your bar is nice, don't forget that a new issue always comes out next month.

Accolades are great. But something much more important drives success and loyalty over time. And unlike traditional *hot spot* thinking, it's not about getting butts in the seats.

It's about keeping them there.

POURING WITH HEART DRIVES REPEAT CUSTOMERS

The best customers are not the biggest spenders. The highest tippers. Or the lowest maintenance. The best customers… are *repeat customers*.

Pouring with Heart is how a bartender brings those repeat customers back.

In 2021, Smallbiztrends.com reported that approximately 65 percent of small business retail stores' revenue is generated from existing customers. Those guests who return after their initial visit. In our bar group, returning customers drive even more of our revenue. And they bring in new customers that can become future regulars.

When you do the math, it's more than impressive. It's an opportunity to rethink what your job behind the bar *actually is.* If a bar's success is determined by its regulars, then before mixology and measurements, your first priority is earning a return visit.

That means that regulars aren't *part* of the job. They *ARE* the job.

On average, regulars spend approximately 50 percent more than new customers. They also tip better. A LOT BETTER.

Five percent more on average than a first-time customer. For example, earning 20 percent instead of 15 percent on $1,000 of sales is the difference between walking with $200 versus $150 in your pocket that night. Multiply that difference across a few shifts a week, and then throughout the rest of the year, and suddenly that extra 5 percent tip from your regulars adds up pretty fast.

Bartenders who neglect regulars as part of their responsibilities are guilty of short-term thinking. And short-term thinking almost never leads to long-term success.

So, how *exactly* does Pouring with Heart drive repeat business?

The National Institute for the Food Service Industry confirmed the number one reason people don't return to a bar—*by a landslide*–is not the product, food, music, or atmosphere. It's because the staff has an attitude of indifference.

In other words, people don't return to a bar when the staff doesn't give a shit.

Though you probably already knew that because you've experienced it yourself.

You've felt that indifference. And you've walked out because the staff didn't give a shit. People want to feel like they matter. Because most of the time…we feel like we don't.

The truth is, the majority of us spend our lives bobbing in and out of different institutions where we feel like we don't *really fucking* matter. We're a nametag wrapped around a big toe the day we enter this world and the day we leave it. From birth, warm in our mother's arms as we begin to bond. And then again in death, cold on some mortician's slab as we begin to rot.

But in between, thanks in part to the deification of *efficiency* in our working world, people are sooner relegated to a number than they are treated as actual people. Branded the way you would a pig. With lipstick and a livestock ID number painted on our ass, so as to make sure all us hogs are in the proper slop bin. Before we are a "Barb" or a "Bob"—to our government—we are a Social Security number. To our insurance company—a policy number. Hell, the local deli only knows you as B-17. But only when you're in line for a half-pound of coleslaw.

So when a human being walks into a bar, the last thing they want to feel like is a fucking number.

They want to feel like they matter.

When a customer walks into a bar for the first time, they have the same look a child does entering a toy store during the holidays. They're fascinated. They want to look around and see things. Taste things. *Feel* things the way human beings need to do from time to time to remember that they are indeed *alive*.

Yes, they may have come in for a cocktail.

But what they really want is to be seen. To be heard.

To be *human*.

And they're getting a chance to be human…*in your bar.*

If you provide your guests with a safe refuge for human connection. If you extend a promise to them that you have their best interests at heart. If you prove that their time spent in your bar is more than transactional.

They will return.

So, if a bartender wants to drive repeat business and build a strong customer base, they must exhibit the opposite of indifference. They've got to Pour with Heart. They've got to avoid the trap of thinking of their customers as credit card numbers. The best bartenders do this. They commit, always, to treating the guest right in front of them as a person.

The legends take it a step further and treat that guest as if they were the *only* person in the room. And those are the bartenders we love.

I'm sure you remember a time at a bar when the staff showed genuine interest in you and your experience. You remember it because you felt warm, valued, and comfortable. I bet you wanted to go back to that bar again. You probably ran to tell your friends about your new favorite hangout. Another benefit of the magic that comes from a bartender that Pours with Heart is that it leaves us—and all our friends—wanting to support that bar again.

Because we know they care about us.

That's as important now as it's ever been in our lifetimes because, let's face it, we live in an age of cynicism with a general lack of trust. As bleak as that sounds, I'm probably still sugarcoating it a bit. Think about it. We have skepticism in our media. Our medical field. Our leaders and politicians. This all adds to a building malaise of uncertainty. Unease and an inability to get comfortable. Like cats in a litter box.

We tiptoe around, hesitant, trying to find the perfect spot to perch, when the truth is that everywhere we look, something's covered in shit.

It hardens us.

We give in to our defenses. Put up walls. Prioritize our needs above others'. It happens so often, and so quickly, that eventually it becomes our new normal. Creating more and more distance between each other.

But on the flip side, when a bartender genuinely cares, when they make a concerted effort to ensure their customers matter, we all stop and take note. It feels so damn good. And the reason it does is because when service comes from the heart, we can feel it inside ours.

It's that infectious.

Primarily because most of us are uncomfortable being warm to new people. We grow up with war-torn hearts, learning at an early age that we should "never trust strangers." This may be sound advice for a lot of us; it's advice meant for our protection. But much like everything else, this kind of social safeguarding also comes at a price.

It shouldn't take courage to truly listen and be there for someone else. Opening our hearts to be present and connect with a stranger shouldn't be considered an act of bravery.

But as long as it is, when someone (like a bartender) does it for us, we feel it tenfold. This warmth, this connectedness we feel when someone *really* hears us, seems to hit on something far beyond our logical understanding.

THE SCIENCE OF THE HEART

First, let's start with some basic facts about the human heart. The heart is the master organ in our body. It's formed first, and it's the last organ to stop when our number is called.

Many ancient cultures, such as the Egyptians, believed there was a strong association between the heart and the soul. Modern science is also starting to support this. According to *The Heart Speaks* by Mimi Guarneri, "Our brain is our source of intellectual intelligence. But modern science has proven that the heart is our emotional intelligence." Emotional intelligence is our ability to empathize and connect with others. If we lack empathy, chances are it's a direct result of us failing to tap into our heart's intelligence.

That's right; I said the heart has intelligence. It actually contains a small brain (neurons) within it, and it thinks and feels independently of the brain in our head. Which explains a lot if you've ever felt compelled to act in a way that was the opposite of your mind's better judgment. In fact, it's the job of those neurons (the brain in our heart) to convert our emotions into instructions for the brain in our head to follow.

Not the other way around.

So many times, our minds say *that's the right job for us. That's the right person for us.* But for whatever reason, *our heart isn't in it.* The heart wins that tug-of-war every time.

Our hearts also have a memory. They remember the important people in our lives we care about. Feelings of love and appreciation send healing instructions throughout our bodies and tell our brain to shower those people with love and attention. The very thought of gratitude can actually make us feel better physically.

But our hearts don't stop there.

It's been proven that patients receiving heart transplants often have accompanying dreams and personal memories from their heart donor. For example, Daniel Levy details in his book, *A Change of Heart,* the story of an eight-year-old girl who received a transplanted heart from a ten-year-old girl who had been murdered. The eight-year-old had clear dreams and memories of the event in question, and even remembered the murderer's name and last words to the victim.

Memories from the eight-year-old girl's new heart eventually put the killer behind bars.

Further, research from Dr. Guarneri in *The Heart Speaks* explains in simple terms how our heart's energy is more powerful than we can comprehend. "The electromagnetic current of the heart is sixty times higher in amplitude than the field of the brain," Guarneri says. "It also emits an energy field five thousand times stronger than the brain's, one that can be measured more than ten feet from the body. To negate the heart is to negate what is essential in ourselves—and in all whom we come in contact with."

Dr. Guarneri's findings inspire us to never discount the power of our hearts. And remember that when a customer sits directly in front of a bartender's well, they are sitting in the middle of the electromagnetic field of that bartender's heart.

If we have the ability to heal others with our hearts, then I can't think of a greater stage to do so than when standing in front of a guest at your bar.

TECHNOLOGY IS CREATING MORE LONELINESS

Technology was supposed to bring us together, but instead, it seems to have found a way to do the opposite. And at an alarming rate, leaving us spending less and less time inside each other's heart radiuses.

We spend insane amounts of time on our mobile phones, social media, and email. Studies show that the average American spends four hours daily on their mobile device, hitting its buttons an incredible 2,600 times per day.

We are addicted to our devices. And that addiction comes at a tremendous cost, taking us away from quality time with our friends, family, and loved ones. Connection with the people we love is so damn essential for our own happiness, *but even more so* for our sanity.

I'm guilty of this cell phone addiction myself. To get away, I force myself to switch off my technology when I'm around my kids. In order to write this book, I had to set aside time without the distraction of technology; otherwise, I would have never finished.

Furthermore, there is tremendous data showing that the internet and social media make us lonelier. Two-plus hours a day on social media, ironically, leaves people feeling isolated. Similarly, the more time a person spends on Facebook, the greater their depression level. Not to mention the ruthless, disturbing behavior allowed to run wild on social media.

The amount of shaming online is out of control. As you may know, teenage suicide rates have skyrocketed as a result of online bullying associated with social media.

And technology doesn't care.

Because neither humanity nor trust are variables of the online algorithm designed to keep us engaged. Which is why I laugh when people suggest I should replace my bartenders with robots.

A soulless machine cannot, and will not, ever tend bar in one of our family's bars.

That goes against everything a bar should stand for. Frankly, it's the job of any great bartender to *avoid* acting like a robot.

I'd quit the bar business and walk away barefoot and broke, with my last bourbon in hand, before I gave a bartender's job away to a damn machine.

The main reason we go to a bar is to interact with others and enjoy the good times that are born of it. Otherwise, we can just drink at home. And do so for *much* cheaper, by the way.

The artificial intelligence (AI) revolution is here. Obsessed with the goal of making our lives more *convenient*, technology relieves us of more and more of our intellectual duties. This levels the intellectual playing field, effectively driving the stock of human intellectual value down.

There is no value assigned to the smartest person in the room when the smartest person in the room is Google.

Fortunately, the silver lining to our intellectual value sinking is that it makes room for a new commodity to soar.

Emotional intelligence.

Those who can connect well with others, are empathetic toward others, and listen to others. Emotional intelligence resides in the one place we have left that's spared from technology.

In our hearts.

Because of that, as long as emotional intelligence remains untethered to a machine, it will be the true gauge by which our value in society is determined.

I've drunk in thousands of bars in my life. Some I owned. Most, I just took over a bar stool for the night like everyone else in the joint. Over the years, no matter the bar, no matter the booze behind it, the *best* bartenders always had the same characteristic in common: they all tapped into their hearts to drive connection.

Now, it's your turn.

To tap into your heart and show off your emotional intelligence. And the best part is, it's wired into all of our DNA. Tapping into your heart is innate in all of us. It's part of who we are and how humanity has survived for hundreds of thousands of years.

In fact, science encourages us to do so.

The brain releases four chemicals that either reward us for behavior or protect us from danger. These chemicals—dopamine, serotonin, oxytocin, and cortisol—directly impact our survival, not just as individuals but as a community and overall species as well.

DOPAMINE
Dopamine is a neurotransmitter our body uses to motivate us to seek pleasure from food and breeding. It's a chemical

messenger designed to give us a positive feeling that enables us to feel good about those basic actions.

But the problem with pleasure signals is they're usually temporary. The more temporary the feeling of pleasure we receive, the more we tend to chase it. And that chase can become extremely addicting. So much so that we have become quite good at finding artificial ways of dousing our brains with this chemical, such as using and abusing drugs, gambling, smoking, watching porn, and eating junk food.

We also get dopamine from text messaging, email, Facebook likes, and social media followers. In fact, we've become such a dopamine-dependent society that companies have dedicated billions to strategize how to use our dopamine addiction against us.

Though you might first think of big tobacco companies when discussing this sort of thing, the products from some of the most successful dopamine marketers out there are already stocked up in your very own kitchen pantry.

Foods loaded with instant dopamine boosters like high fructose corn syrup. Hell, according to some studies, sugar is just as addictive as cocaine.

According to author Simon Sinek, all addictions are basically dopamine addictions. The more society attaches itself to digital dependency—for example, "smartphones" keeping us stuck in a constant dopamine loop—the more we see soaring rates of depression.

SEROTONIN

Serotonin is the natural mood stabilizer released in our body that rewards us for working together. This "happy chemical" was important to early man's survival, as hunting as a team worked out better for us when fighting against much bigger foes. Taking on the proverbial (or actual) saber-tooth tiger alone rarely ended well.

Working collaboratively has allowed us to build modern education, transportation, technology, and medicine. Dopamine may have been intended to be constructive for us on an individual level, but serotonin is designed to be constructive for us on a collective level.

Serotonin is also known as a selfless chemical because we are rewarded with it when we take care of *others*. The amazing thing is that we also receive it when someone does something selfless for *us*.

When a bartender is Pouring with Heart, they are actively taking care of someone else. Which means that on top of a cocktail, the customer also receives a shot of serotonin on the house. We naively think the bar guest is in a great mood because of the booze they're sucking down. But the truth is, the science of serotonin is at work.

Also, because of the rewarding nature of the chemical, when a bartender actively looks out for their customer, they not only generate a dose of serotonin for the stranger across the bar but also receive a dose themselves.

OXYTOCIN

Oxytocin is also known as the love chemical. It rewards us for loving other people and being loved. Oxytocin is triggered during desired physical contact and sexual intimacy. It also rewards us for nurturing our babies and our mates.

Without oxytocin and serotonin, our lives feel lonely, callous, and cold.

According to Sinek, the oxytocin and serotonin hormones are both "selfless chemicals [that] are the key to giving us a feeling of belonging, and without them we feel isolated and unconnected with others."

So not only are these chemicals the keys to prolonged happiness, but they also keep us together through difficult circumstances.

When you're high on oxytocin, you'll do almost anything for the person in your life triggering it. Under its spell, you'll find yourself doing things for others, almost instinctively, that you wouldn't normally do on your own.

I can attest to that. I used to be much more of a selfish prick about twenty-one years ago. Before I had kids. Now that I'm a father of two, I'd gladly take a bullet for either one of them.

Without thinking, most of us would step in front of any danger heading for our beautiful children. The love connection brought on by oxytocin gives you something *that* special.

A priority outside of yourself.

CORTISOL

Cortisol is a chemical that is released when we are scared or stressed. When we were Neanderthals, it was meant to warn us of danger. To flood us when we were being chased by a giant predator.

But in today's crazy world of sensory overload and sensationalized news, we get hits of cortisol all the time. It drives up our heart rate and is a major cause of modern stress and anxiety. Because, well, in short:

Bad news and cortisol sell, baby.

In the days of early civilization, a hit of cortisol was temporary. It came and went with the danger, which allowed us to recover from the adrenaline generated in our body that we used to help us escape the danger. When we're inundated with cortisol, however, we lose the ability to determine the difference between real danger and fake news.

Not only that, we become over-adrenalized. We're high-strung, tense, and ready to lose our shit at the drop of a hat. Human beings are meant to be creatures of a peaceful nature. We shouldn't need to be prepared for a fight every five minutes.

It's unnatural.

Maybe the worst part of having cortisol pumping through our system is that it inhibits serotonin and oxytocin flow, which blocks the feeling of love and happiness in our lives. This increase in stress and decrease in happiness leads to things like depression. Inflammation. High blood pressure. Cancer. Heart disease. The list goes on.

Subjecting us to not only a shorter life span but a lesser quality one at that.

A bartender, however, on any given shift, has the rare opportunity to help work against this trend. Knowing that their guests are walking into the bar overstimulated, over-sensationalized, and chock-full of cortisol, Pouring with Heart can help chill a bar guest the fuck out.

Steve Robbins, one of our operations directors, said this about how to treat people in a bar: "It's up to us to do the best we can to give hard-working people the best place to feel safe and have a good time (and let off some steam). Life's a bitch. You just got to recognize each other for the suffering bastards we are on this rock and take care of one another."

Robbins has a hell of a way with words. His sentiment sums up *exactly* why we need to Pour with Heart. Again, if all these hard-working people needed was a drink, they would get it at home. People come to a bar for much more than that.

THE LIGHT AT THE END OF THE TUNNEL
DOESN'T HAVE TO BE A TRAIN

The more serotonin we share, the better. The more oxytocin in the room, the more it proves we're doing something right. I'm damn proud that people meet their soulmates in our spots. It feels great to get invitations to staff and customers' weddings, knowing they first fell in love inside our doors.

When an entire bar staff is Pouring with Heart, you can feel the magic. The serotonin is flowing, and almost everyone is caught up in its spell. But make no mistake, it's hard work. Putting your heart and soul into being of service to others isn't easy, and furthermore, it takes practice.

It's difficult to stay focused on others when we're so easily distracted by our own personal bullshit. Not to mention, it's awkward at first. But like most new things worth trying—*push through the awkwardness*. It's just a speed bump on the road to a rewarding bartending career.

Danny Meyer is arguably the most respected restaurateur in the country. He's discovered the real secret of the restaurant business—and it isn't having the greatest food or being the hottest, trendiest restaurant.

Meyer said, "My appreciation of the power of hospitality, and the desire to harness it, is the greatest contributor to my success." Danny's biggest accomplishments do not stem from the restaurants he built but instead from the understated value of being of service to guests along the way.

CHAPTER TWO

WHY WORK IN A BAR

*"We may have all come on different ships.
But we are on the same boat now."*
—Martin Luther King, Jr.

Τ his book was really hard to write. I'm not much of a *front man*. I've always preferred to be behind the scenes and let others be the ones to take the stage. Own the spotlight.

Like my dad.

Ed Moses. He *was* the spotlight. He was a social rock star, the kind that came alive when the lights were at their brightest. And people loved him for it.

But that wasn't me.

I've always had an inner confidence. That was never a problem because I've always known my shit. But speaking in front of a crowd, I fall apart. It feels like I'm melting in front of the audience. My voice cracks, my forehead sweats, and pretty soon I'm a puddle behind the podium.

The spotlight makes me uncomfortable. I'm afraid of exposing my nervous, shy, awkward self. Of feeling vulnerable.

I know I'm not the only one who feels this way, thanks to friends and similar souls who have shared their stories with me about this kinda thing. Yet despite knowing this, still, in my mind, I'm ashamed. I'm ashamed of my awkwardness. Even though I'd say to others…it's nothing to be ashamed of.

Falsely or not, it feels like a weakness.

It's difficult for men in our culture to admit they feel weak. Most of us fear weakness more than we fear our own death.

After all, our culture loves a good show of strength. It likes its men to swallow their feelings. Because why acknowledge weakness when you can repress it?

The irony about strength is that it is, by definition, born of weakness. It's the weakness that makes us strong. So, if you're never weak, well, you can finish the sentence.

I've repressed my fair share of weakness. Avoided countless interviews and speaking engagements over the years. And all this in spite of a growing reputation as one of the biggest bar operators in the country.

A mogul, they said.

Sometimes I wonder who they're talking about. The image of me, projected onto me, is one that's diametrically opposed to the person I still see in the mirror.

Back to fear and loathing weakness.

You'd think I'd compensate for not liking public speaking by being really good with words. Wrong again. I was never much of a writer, so sharing my thoughts and an early draft of this book was terrifying. They're just words on a page, but somehow, they find themselves creeping into your self-worth. In fact, they get so intertwined you can't tell the difference between how your manuscript is received and how worthwhile, or worthless, of a person you are.

IT HAPPENED IN A BAR

I've always admired how my father could put such bold work out there and be so comfortable. Disclaimer: My father would be absolutely nuts before his shows, though. Hanging and rehanging his artwork dozens of times before the opening like a madman on Adderall. Sometimes, still rehanging work even as people made their way inside the gallery. He was striving for perfection. And doing it out of fear of failure and unworthiness.

Well, we had that in common.

I had to find some courage. I had to overcome my fear and find some comfort in the spotlight. Since I seldom bare my soul outside of it. Even more seldomly in a book. There's no taking anything back after it's published.

This book was the outcome of my growth. But it wasn't the catalyst. Overcoming my fear of vulnerability didn't happen between these pages.

It happened in a bar.

An uncomfortable, clumsy kid with a pimply, lanky image of myself branded into the back of my retinas. That was me. And though summer camp and college did their best to socialize me, they never absolved me of that pressing feeling inside.

The feeling of being socially awkward forever.

And moreover, the shame of that feeling. A ball and chain around my neck, suffocating every attempt I made to put myself out there.

I didn't know what it was at the time, but sitting there, sipping on something at my local dive, I unknowingly became part of something else. The courageous, I would call them, brave enough to open up to total strangers every night.

Bar people inspired me. Their nerve helped me learn that we all have fucking imperfections, and sometimes, those imperfections aren't so hideous.

Often, they're beautiful.

It was bar people who helped me realize that. Those sitting beside me. Those serving me. Those who brought me out of my shell. Bar folks listened to my crazy dreams of one day crusading across the country in the name of bar culture and historic dives. Bar men and women gave me access to a fuel I did not know I had.

So, I continued to go back to the bar. As I gained courage, I could see further, and clearer, past this world's veil. The watering hole was a place of community. People helping people. And when you looked around, one thing stood out to me among the crowd.

I was surrounded by a sea of misfits. No wonder I was so welcome here.

Because as it turns out, misfits aren't misfits amongst misfits. And furthermore, as Dr. King said, no matter how we got here, we were all on the same boat now.

A PLACE TO CALL HOME

My dad didn't fit into conventional America. He was told art school would be a dead end. And his misfit friends would be the death of him. Looking back, these friends of his weren't so much misfits as they were masters of their universe. They didn't think twice about making money. They didn't have room to pursue that *and their passion* at the same time.

These artists were my initiation into subculture and people living on the fringe of society. Those who don't fit the traditional mold but can open their minds outside their comfort zone. They inspired me to have confidence in thinking counterculture over mainstream culture and challenging the status quo.

What's more, interesting people like this are usually the best at connecting with others. They're passionate. They're emotional. Complex and curiously layered.

In most businesses, the misfit is the fringe player. Constantly struggling to fit in with the team. Always up for review. Talked about behind their back and conveniently uninvited to the team lunch.

But in a bar, the misfit is the team captain.

Because of that, the bar will always be a safe place where us misfits from all over can come together and find one another. More than just a place we can feel at home.

A place we can all call home.

THE BAR BUSINESS IS COMPLETELY MISUNDERSTOOD
I take a lot of pride in my home.

So when I hear people say bartending is something you do when you can't hack it in the real world, that the bar business is a great place for a temporary gig until you get a "real job," I think to myself:

Fuck them.

And that's it, really. I won't give any more credence to those ignorant, short-sighted slights. What I will do, instead, is lean on my twenty-five years in the business and share with you the experiences of our bar group that proves them wrong.

I'll show you the other side of these stigmas. Unpack the proof of value, merit, and the nobility of working in a bar. We'll talk about pride. We'll talk about honor. We'll discuss the fruits of being of service to your fellow man.

You know, Pouring with Heart.

And then you can decide for yourself whether the critics' arguments carry any weight.

THE ANTIDOTE FOR HUMAN INTERACTION

Many predict that millions of careers are in jeopardy as AI and robots are expected to replace workers across a lot of industries. But despite modern technology, the bar business is going to thrive and create great jobs because it has a human factor that can't be replaced. Service-oriented careers, in general, will grow even more stable as technology progresses.

Jeff Weiner, the Executive Chairman of LinkedIn, one of the world's authorities on careers, said that "as powerful as AI will ultimately become and is becoming, we're still a ways away from computers being able to replicate and replace human interaction and touch. So, there's a wonderful incentive for people to develop these skills because those jobs are going to be more stable for a longer period of time."

Damn right!

You can't have a real emotional interaction on Amazon. Smart devices may be able to perform human tasks on command, but they will never have the ability to empathize with an actual human being. Technology will never truly know what it's like to walk in our shoes.

Bars thrive when the staff accepts everyone who walks through their doors and makes it their goal to be completely of service to them. The internet, FaceTime, WhatsApp, Zoom, and social media in general are also designed to be of service to us. But many of these services come at a price. While most of these apps work together, connecting our personal needs, they're also simultaneously disconnecting us from something else.

Real, human interaction.

We are facing a crisis of isolation in America. And no one suffers worse than the youth of our nation. Our children don't just experience isolation now—they're born into it! It's where they live. Consumed by and often simultaneously parented by whatever device is charged.

And though the youth may shoulder a heavy and unjust load, we are all vulnerable to the backlash of modern conveniences. Our pleasure centers have been rewired and short-circuited by the unlimited dopamine fix…after fix…after fix…siphoning the human connection we come into this world longing for, one screen at a time.

Smallbiztrends.com revealed a 2020 study that showed 66 percent of Americans check their phones an average of 160 times each day. If we do the math on that, that's roughly once every six to seven-and-a-half minutes.

Imagine being at a bar and ordering a drink every six to seven-and-a-half minutes. Not only would you develop a reputation as a rip-roaring drunk, but you and your distinguished BAC would be respectfully cut off and likely given an escort out the door.

Think about the addictive nature of a limitless dopamine drip in your pocket. Any product you desire is available through one app or another to be dropped on your doorstep in a day. All you need is an itch and a click of a button.

What you don't need…is any kind of human interaction.

So, as life becomes more "convenient" for the average person in America, it's also becoming more lonely. How lonely? Harvard

University suggests the number of people that consider themselves lonely has ballooned to 60 percent in this country.

That's almost 200 million people.

Fortunately, there's an antidote for this. It's called camaraderie and a sense of belonging.

Two things that come alive when bartenders are Pouring with Heart.

IT'S NOT ROCKET SCIENCE. IT'S A CONVERSATION.

For some, there's an intimidation factor that prevents us from working behind a bar. Maybe it's the giant whiskey walls breathing down your neck. Bottles representing countries all over the world with their precious, first-place science fair experiments housed inside. How do you keep track of all the information? The names. The distillers' names. The names of the distilleries!?

Highland. Lowland. Bourbon. Tennessee. Islay. Peated. Sherry. Caribbean rum.

And American Oak.

What does it all mean?

Forget the whiskey for a second. Maybe you find yourself behind the well in a high-volume cocktail bar. Staring back

at you are a litany of spirits, liqueurs, bitters, fruits, and garnishes. Each available ingredient representing hundreds of
permutations of the different cocktails you'll be expected to
execute. You know them well—you've probably studied for
nights on end, scribbling recipes across flashcards you might
still be holding onto in your back pocket.

But now the temperature in the bar rises with each new group
of friends that makes its way to you. They're thirsty, and
they've got *a lot* of options.

The time for flashcards has passed. You're behind the wheel
now, left to rely on your newly formed intimate knowledge
of recipes and measurements, and your ability to make
taste-worthy concoctions in a timely fashion before the line
grows long and your customers grow angry.

You cycle through the fundamentals. Spirit forward. Sours.
Highballs. Juleps. Smashes. Tikis. Martinis. Manhattans and
Fizzes.

Remember the rules so you don't spoil someone's night with
poor craftsmanship, or worse, the wrong ingredients.

God forbid you shake an aromatic.

Seems like a lot of pressure, right? Well, the best bartenders in
the business would disagree. Take this passage from *This Must
Be the Place: Memoirs of Montparnasse by Jimmie "the Barman"
Charters* by Morrill Cody, for example:

Almost anyone can learn to mix drinks accurately and fast. That is the least of it. I have always believed success behind the bar comes from an ability to understand the man or woman I am serving, to enter into his joys or woes, make him feel the need of me as a person rather than a servant.

Making drinks, as Jimmie "the Barman" said back in 1937 and countless other legendary bartenders would still attest to today, is the least of it.

The myth, the mystery, the mad science of it all, looks over-whelming from afar. But trust me, the day you start behind the bar is the day the fog is lifted.

You'll learn all the tricks. All the trade secrets. The extremely simplified categorization of cocktails and spirits. And how nearly every cocktail you'll ever need to know is largely just a variation based on a dozen original, classic recipes.

We want to keep the art of bartending simple. It behooves us to teach systems we can all learn and master easily. This way we can all do the job and provide a comfortable consistency when we do it.

And yes, there are some hallowed juices out there. Whiskeys, mezcals, and other such spirits may be soaked in history. But most of their stories are told by people just like yourself. Their histories and creation methods aren't reserved for the few. They're open books, just like anything else. Easy to learn about when you digest it over time.

And most of the time, you don't have to know *everything*. This just in: people like alcohol. They also like stories. A little information goes a long way when you're sharing with a guest. Also, remember when you're with your guest, it's not a transaction.

It's a conversation.

So if they ask for something wildly exotic like a "Slow Comfortable Screw Against the Wall," you have options. You can look them in the eye and respond honestly: "I have no idea how to make that." Then readjust your position: "But what I can do is offer to make this cocktail (insert a drink you can crush) that I think will make your night."

Challenge accepted! If I'm a guest, I've long forgotten about the Slow Comfortable Screw Against the Wall...Against the Wall with Satin Pillows...and Against the Wall in the Dark Side of Mexico City.

Yes, those are all real cocktails, each with just one or two variations to their base.

You can also ask the guest how to make the cocktail. This is allowed, believe it or not. It doesn't show weakness in your profession. Instead, it's a great opportunity to show humility and that you're there to support them before serving your own ego. Even if you haven't committed their eccentric taste to memory, they'll respect your honesty and enthusiasm to get there.

"Ultimately, what a guest is looking for is friendly and efficient service, and a chance to forget about a bad day, or to celebrate a great day, with a good fucking drink. Too many of our peers have gotten too caught up in the perceived importance of their drinks and their status among their peers."

—Jeff Hollinger, bar owner and author,
***The Art of the Bar*, 2014**

And if neither of the first two options works, there's always a cocktail book handy. Once you have the basic understanding of how ingredients come together as instruments in a symphony, you can pick up any sheet of music and conduct with confidence.

Again, it's the things that seem overwhelming about a bar that actually become the easiest to do. Conversely, it's the simple steps we take for granted that are the most difficult for some to grasp.

The intangibles. Being completely of service to the person directly in front of you.

Pouring with Heart.

That's the real challenge. Connecting with guests. Reading the room and learning how to put your community at ease. To offer them delicious, well-balanced cocktails, yes. But more than that, a feeling they can leave smiling about—and *keep* smiling about—until they return.

You don't need flashcards for that.

THE BEST BARS PROVIDE ACCEPTANCE

By now, we know the job is less about the objective things we see from the outside. Cocktail recipes and mixology. Mustache grooming and vests. However important they may be on their own, they all take a considerable backseat to creating an environment worth drinking in for your customers. Good bars are good at this. Stimulating things like camaraderie and a sense of belonging, both of which really only boil down to one thing.

Acceptance.

Young adults have few outlets left to experience public human interaction. If not live music festivals or bars, where do they get it? College? Their first internship? Though the latter two may be filled with people and human interaction, they're also cluttered with competition. Someone is always out-studying you for a better grade in college. Someone is always vying for the position promised at the end of your internship.

Music festivals don't pit concertgoers against one another, a likely reason behind their globally skyrocketing sales over the last decade. In 2018, *Billboard* reported that more than 32 million Americans attended at least one music festival. That year there were over eight hundred music festivals, with attendees coughing up hundreds of dollars for tickets and each traveling an average of 903 miles to get there.

But even music festivals have their warts. I won't get into the infamous STD statistics released post-major music festivals. But I will comment on the cost and availability issues that present themselves. Festivals are pricey, and they aren't something you can visit daily after work.

Bars, on the other hand, might be the last rodeo in terms of building camaraderie with people in your community. A sanctum you can visit regularly without the weight of a tremendous price tag afterward.

Bars provide a vital respite away from work and home. The biggest reason? They are one of the last destinations available to us where people are still truly accepted for who they are. Particularly in these isolating times, having a central hub that accepts its community—across cultures—allows us to reconnect with our humanity. To lower our defense mechanisms and let in new people, laughs, and conversation.

I am not the only one who sees bars this way.

In 2018, bar sales in the US racked up an insane $26.7 billion. As the internet, our mobile devices, and social media continue to take over our lives, the bar business is going to grow in almost every American city. Because it's a natural regression to the mean.

Meaning, it's hallowed ground we can rely on to rehabilitate those 200 million lonely souls and rekindle human interaction and relationships.

Acceptance is transformative in people's lives. It alleviates stress and anxiety.

Warms us. Lightens us.

We feel special when we feel welcomed. When a bartender remembers our name. Smiles at us and rewards us with our favorite pint, frosty and full, just because we made it in that night. We don't need to pass a test or meet a deadline. All we have to do is get comfortable in our seat while we wait for the foam to settle.

Goddamn if that doesn't make me thirsty.

I've witnessed the acceptance bars provide communities, bringing them together in the most challenging of environments. It's a powerful thing that impacts so many people.

When you choose to work in a bar, you get access to that power each shift.

But it doesn't end there.

WANT DIVERSITY? LOOK TO YOUR LOCAL BAR

If things like diversity and inclusivity are important to you, then you'll be happy to know the bar business promotes both in spades.

As I've said before, bar families come from all walks of life. We're misfits, outsiders, the kind of people you can't "place."

The more diverse and inclusive a bar, the more it reflects its community. Let's use a popular bar game for an analogy here. Think of a bar's employees as darts for a second. If all our darts were snug inside the bullseye, we'd be pretty stale as an organization—and worse, we'd be highly expendable for a guest with access to Zagat or Yelp.

Predictability may be valuable in a customer's day to day, but it is just the opposite when it comes to their escape.

In essence, in the bar world, the further spread out the darts are, the better the board looks.

To clarify, the best bars don't just accept everyone in terms of customers; they also do so in terms of employment. They operate from a standpoint that better human rights equals better human progress, and better overall human goodness.

At my bars, we have zero tolerance for racial or sexual discrimination. It's simply unacceptable.

To me, bars are one of the most American of institutions that exist. They're completely accessible, democratic, and open to everyone—because being of service to others is something inherent and open to all of humanity.

Martin Luther King Jr. said it best: "Everybody can be great... because anybody can serve. You don't have to have a college degree...You only need a heart full of grace. A soul generated by love."

You definitely don't need a college education to be in this business. Most of my leadership team doesn't have one. But they damn sure tap into their hearts with souls generated by love to be completely of service to others.

Diversity of people and its ripple effect truly makes the bar business compelling by constantly leading to new and different perspectives.

In this business, we accept and love each other as family. Your race, gender, and sexual orientation shouldn't be obstacles. They should be celebrated. And if you find yourself at a place where that's *not* the case, then how else can I say it?

You're probably at the wrong bar.

The right bar embraces diversity in its family and knows their team is better off because of it. Folks from all walks of life building better bars, together, is a beautiful thing.

Another great quote from Steve Robbins puts it this way: "What I love about our culture is that we might all come from different backgrounds, places, religions, and ethnicities, and no matter our gender, regardless of our backgrounds, we share the common goal of getting better and improving our bars. We are all accepted and loved as part of our bar family."

WORKING AT A BAR = AMAZING FRIENDSHIPS

Maybe one of the biggest benefits of working in the bar industry is the amazing times you'll have and the great friends you'll make along the way. The spirit of hospitality runs through bars, live music venues, restaurants, and hotels. And it doesn't just apply to those across the bar. A lot of that energy comes from within.

People in the hospitality business have a way of smelling it on each other. Once inside, you become like kindred spirits. Often you'll find yourself getting "hooked up" (e.g., free stuff, the best table) at restaurants and bars in your area. You also often get special access to concerts and sporting events. If you are single, you are opening up the opportunity to find sex, romance, and even your soulmate. You will get to know people in your town faster than you would ever imagine.

And they'll get to know you too.

Bartenders do two things every night. One, they host the party. And two, they control the booze. That means they're in charge of the room and the most popular people in it. Which usually extends outside of the room because, let's face it, charisma doesn't quit at two a.m.

As a bartender, you're a cocktail-slinging confession booth for the craziest and most uninhibited folks in town. It's a big reason why whenever there's a local party happening or an awesome new bar/restaurant opening, the best bartenders in the city warrant an invite.

I'm sure you've had your fair share of dead-end jobs. I've worked in many jobs, and most were a fucking nightmare. The kind where no one gave a shit about each other, everyone was out for themselves, and they all had an agenda.

When I worked in the financial business, I made some decent money, but I felt like I was going spiritually bankrupt. No soul—and no thanks.

The bar business is for people who are sick of conforming to the typical corporate work environment. We don't care if people have piercings, tattoos, and wild haircuts.

We want you to do...*you*.

Do your thing. Be yourself. Loving people for who they are, and not how they look, is typical of bar cultures across the country. It's this acceptance and the good times that come along with it—arguably because of it—that leads to a strong sense of job satisfaction.

Elsewhere, job satisfaction is at its lowest level ever recorded—and declining annually—because people don't feel valued and fulfilled at work. About 50 percent of the workforce can't stand their jobs. And shockingly, Simon Sinek tells us, *over* 50 percent of people, when asked if they'd be happier if they were unemployed (rather than continue on at their current job), said "yes."

The advantage of the bar business is that you can be highly valued by your bar guests and your bar family. Also, well-managed venues tend to treat their bar staffers like royalty. That's hard to find in corporate America.

Not to mention, bartenders that are of service to their guests are also financially rewarded by being so.

Pouring with Heart leads to better tips.

BAR BUSINESS = GOOD $$$

Bartenders generally make good money. As you may know, American bartenders make minimum wage plus tips. Tips typically range from 15 to 20 percent of the bill. A decent bartender should be able to ring in $1,500/night when the bar is busy, so you can see how tips can add up quickly. And how $300 a night in your pocket is well within reach in a decent bar.

In a busy bar, bartenders make career-level pay (without the college loans to pay back), while only working an average of thirty hours per week. Compensation varies widely for management positions, but they usually come with more stable income, health insurance, and profit-sharing.

We're talking solid pay while having a blast and hanging with the best people in town.

Also, bars are resilient.

Unlike the high failure rate of full-service restaurants and nightclubs, bars rarely go out of business due to their solid business model. Bars keep their lights on with low overhead and good profit margins on alcohol. Not to mention a bar that is Pouring with Heart never goes out of style because it is always attracting and retaining customers.

Plus, bars are recession-proof. Folks drink in good times and in bad. In fact, people typically drink more alcohol when times are the toughest.

Because they know their local bartender is going to help them through it.

Acceptance. Diversity. Inclusion. Opportunity. Fulfillment. And on some nights, a good bartender can make more than a damn doctor.

Those critical of bartending are slow to bring up these merits. It's not their fault. Most of them have never done the job. And thus, do not know what they *do not know*.

However, the most important thing I'd like *you to know*…is this.

You're "allowed" to get a job in a bar. Whether you're college-educated or not. Whether you feel like you belong or not. Whether your parents tell you they respect the choice or not. Whether others deem it beneath you, or beneath them, or not.

Misfits like us with our tattoos, music, hairdos, and hangovers…can take a job in the bar business. And not just as a "temporary gig." As a *real job*. A job you can grow to love.

A job you can brag about. A job that you show up early for because you're excited to start.

A job you can look in the mirror after each shift and be proud you've earned.

CHAPTER THREE

AMERICA STARTED IN A GODDAMN BAR

(And Other Reasons to Choose a Career in This Business)

"Whether you think you can, or you think you can't—you're right."
—Henry Ford

Some people think bartending is a shitty job. Well, let me tell you something about this *shit job*. It's been a staple of our culture since we forged our very independence.

Americans like to drink. They like to come together for drinks…and be served. That's something we can all agree on.

Where some people differ is in the nobility behind those doing the serving. Unfortunately, the court of public opinion hasn't always been kind.

The National Opinion Research Center (NORC), reported

on the value the public placed on different jobs in America. They dubbed it "occupational prestige," a metric asked by the Census Bureau at the turn of the 1990 decade, measured between a score of 1 to 100.

No surprise, some of the higher scores included clergy members (68.9), judges (71.4), and physicians (86.1). Those in hospitality fared much worse.

At the time, "bartender" scored a crowd-pleasing *24.5*. Sandwiched comfortably between parking lot attendants (21.2) and "garbage men" (27.7).

Twenty-five years later, in 2014, CareerCast.com posted their annual report on the top 200 jobs in America, ranked best to worst. This report came well after the whiskey boom of the early 2000s and the corresponding rise in popularity of handcrafted cocktails across the service industry.

All that said, would it surprise you to know "bartender" still ranked in the bottom 50 jobs from the top 200 list?

Well, it didn't.

In fact, "bartender" didn't make the list at all.

Despite more than 580,000 Americans holding a bartending job that year.

What is the disconnect?

I believe working behind a bar to be a badge of honor. More people confide in their bartender than they do their own spouse. Their priest. Their president.

Heavy is the head that pours the *Crown*.

People don't often let their guards down. But they do in a bar.

In this society, we need our bartenders. We rely on our bartenders. And what the court of public opinion—per a Census Bureau report card—doesn't tell you...

Is that we love our bartenders.

This chapter is dedicated to those behind the bar brave enough to love back. Despite the disconnect that exists between our love of bartenders and our lack of appreciation for them.

Here's the tricky part.

Changing the disconnect does not come from changing the court of public opinion. It comes from us. From fellow bartenders.

From within.

The public doesn't need to know our history. But *we* do.

Because it's only by understanding our past that we can shed the hackneyed snakeskin of bartending as a lesser-valued occupation. When we realize how special we are, how important we are, and how valuable we've been and will always be…

Our shoulders straighten. Our chests swell a bit.

For many of us, for the first time, we can see the proof in the pudding of what I promised you in the last chapter:

That bartending is a worthy job.

An occupation that comes with a sense of pride, that gives you reason to press your vest and show up to work on Friday night ready to kick some ass. But more than that, this industry can offer you something most people don't realize is even possible in this business.

A career.

A strange word for mere slingers of cocktails, is it not?

Careers should be reserved for grandiose trades like lawyering, computer engineering, or marital therapizing. The words "career" and "bar" don't generally end up in the same sentence.

The truth is, whether you think you can or you can't have a career as a bartender, either way, as Henry Ford said, *you're right.*

But before you make that choice, it's important that you're drawing from a full deck.

There are a few things every newcomer to this business should know. Hell, even the vets deserve a listen. We can all benefit from a better understanding of the true foundation of bartending.

What we're *really* doing when we slide drinks across the bar top. This chapter is a celebration. A recognition of how cool it is to be part of the bartender bloodline in this country.

In case I haven't been crystal fucking clear, you're part of something special.

Get this straight: you are not part of the help.

You are part of *history*.

And the inspiring tradition that *shaped* our history.

LET'S GO WAY BACK
Like, to the Stone Age. When drinking alcohol first began.

"From the rituals of the Stone Age, the mind-altering properties of alcohol have fired our creativity and fostered the development of language, the arts, and religion. There's good evidence from all over the world that alcoholic beverages are important to human culture...drinking is such an integral part of our humanity."

–Patrick McGovern, archaeologist, *National Geographic*, 2017

Alcohol has been around a *long* time. And for good reason. Not only has it been fueling human creativity since we could stand upright, but due to its connection to language, the arts, and religion, alcohol could be credited for setting liftoff to our civilization.

"People were imbibing alcohol long before they invented writing. The story of humanity's love affair with alcohol goes back to a time before farming...Our taste for tipple may be a hardwired evolutionary trait that distinguishes us from most other animals...our ape ancestors started eating fermented fruits on the forest floor, and that made all the difference. We're preadapted for consuming alcohol."

**—Nathaniel Dominy, biological anthropologist
at Dartmouth College**

Simply put, we were born to drink.

That's not to say drinking is for *everyone*. It's not. Opinions on the subject run the gamut. Some believe alcohol is an evil substance and, if anything, a blight on humanity. Others will swear to you that getting a stiff drink after a hard day's work is nothing short of a religious experience.

This isn't a book meant to argue the merits/evils of the sauce, whether or not people should drink, or how much we should or shouldn't drink. It's simply to explain there is an anthropological reason that we do.

There is abundant evidence that the invention of beer triggered the end of man's nomadic lifestyle and the beginning of towns and modern civilization.

In a *National Geographic* article published in 2019, McGovern said:

> *Anthropologists debate which came first, bread or beer. I think it was beer: it's easier to make, more nutritious, and has a mind-altering effect. These were incentives for hunter-gatherers to settle down and domesticate grain. In the process they set up the first permanent villages and broke down social boundaries between groups. The beginnings of civilization were spurred on by fermented beverages.*

Alcohol is rooted in the development of mankind. And as mankind evolved, so did our DNA. Years of celebrating and entertaining one another with beer, wine, champagne, and spirits have left us genetically predisposed to enjoy—*and endure*–alcohol.

Which brings up a very important caveat.

We may have been born to drink, but we were not born to drink *alone*.

Not with our hard wiring for connection.

More important than finding alcohol, to many of us, is seeking out places to imbibe it. We have a very human, dutiful desire to share booze with others. This stems from our need for connection. Whereas drinking alone might leave you drunk, *drinking together* brings forth an intoxication of camaraderie, togetherness, and friendship among the group.

Alcohol and bars make for an operatic marriage.

They're emotional. Passionate. Always riding the razor's edge.

But it's their consistent, loyal service to humanity that makes them requisite in helping us not only develop our communities, but protect them as well.

So they can survive and grow.

Thank God.

Because it's a tough fucking world out there.

I have a hunch that's the *deeper* reason why alcohol and bars have played such an important role in the development of modern civilization.

Because bars don't just welcome the public. They're a refuge for the public.

For most of us, that's all we need. A safehouse. A place to congregate and be together. To experience some shelter from the storm.

Of course, I'm well aware bars might not always have the best reputation.

But I'll say this. I've learned a hell of a lot more in a bar than I ever did in any classroom.

More about respect, love, and faith sitting on a barstool than I ever did sitting in a pew.

I've experienced the bewitching swell that forges strangers into friends. Seen stress relieved among the anxiety-riddled and overworked. And the barriers broken down between those of us with differences over a couple of beers.

After a tough fucking day, bartenders that Pour with Heart provide some of the last safe havens on Earth.

BARS IN THE EARLY UNITED STATES

In the United States, bars started out as taverns and played a key part in early American culture and enterprise. According to Christine Sismondo's illuminating book, *America Walks into a Bar*, America was colonized and expanded via taverns and drinking establishments:

> *In the seventeenth century, taverns became the de-facto center of everyday life since they were the first major building built in each new city. They operated as a town's post office, bulletin board, courtroom, library, and even church. In towns, the local*

tavern and more British-influenced pub (short for public house)
also became a popular meeting place. Taverns and pubs were
the nucleuses of every town. They were also the first places for
everyone to congregate and freely exercise their freedom of speech.

How little things have changed.

But back in the seventeenth century, a lot of us didn't realize
that beer was actually the healthiest drinking option, since
clean water was a rare—and often unavailable—commodity.
It is said that the Mayflower's journey didn't end because of
a lack of rations, sickness, or damage to the vessel.

The Mayflower ran out of beer.

The ship was originally intended to land at the mouth of the
Hudson River, but instead they called it quits and stopped some
two hundred miles short in order to find beer. And that stop?

A little place called Plymouth Rock.

Fast forward a century or so, and taverns were springing up all
over the East Coast. In fact, by the middle of the eighteenth
century, towns were actually being fined for *not* opening a
tavern because they were considered necessary in providing
a public service.

Somewhat surprisingly, most taverns were used for religious
services, with churches rationalizing the idea that "God is

everywhere." Ironically, certain churches would later lead the country into Prohibition and change their tune to something closer to "God is everywhere—except at the end of a bottle."

While this may still be under debate, there's no arguing our country's founding principles began inside of bars.

One of the most defining moments came during a time of great uncertainty for America. When a bunch of poor farmers, crushed by British taxes, didn't know if they would see their independence ever again. Of if they'd survive the onslaught of the King's militia on American soil.

Until Paul Revere got on his goddamn horse and rode like the fucking wind to let those farmers know that "the British were coming."

Revere rode alone, leaving Charleston around eleven p.m. with a lantern and a prayer. In the early, pulse-pounding moments of his trip, Revere was nearly captured by British officers before escaping through the town of Medford. Once safe in Medford, he alerted the town's residents and local militia...

Right after he ordered himself a dram of rum.

Yes, Sismondo reveals that "historians are quick to point out the stop in Medford came with a quick drink of rum. Revere's midnight tipple, they call it."

I don't blame the man.

If he had he been captured, he would have been slain, and much more blood of his countrymen—*our countrymen*—would have been spilled. If we hadn't gotten Revere's heads-up, America as we know it may have never come to fruition.

Feel free to celebrate that the next time you pour yourself a rum.

On the flip side, when the British *did* arrive, Sismondo explains, "their first order of business was to occupy Wright's Tavern, and there, Commander John Pitcairn stepped to the bar and ordered himself a brandy. He also pricked a finger, and dripped some blood into his drink, and offered a toast that rebel (American) blood would be shed that day."

We'd lay that redcoat to rest two months later at the Battle of Bunker Hill.

But Wright's Tavern would go on to survive the Revolutionary War and then serve our countrymen in celebration of the independence that so many "rebels" died for.

Long before the victory was celebrated, the plans for the American Revolution were hatched on these taverns' bar tops. But they were also communicated to the masses there. American patriots would flood to bars to hear inspired rhetoric read aloud. Rallying cries by poets standing on top of those bars fueled those farmers to fight.

"O ye that love mankind! Ye that dare oppose, not only the tyranny, but the tyrant, stand forth!"

**–Thomas Paine, revolutionary leader and poet,
author of *Common Sense***

Thomas Jefferson even wrote the first draft of the Declaration of Independence in a Philadelphia pub called the Indian Queen Tavern. Just Tom, a blank sheet of parchment, and a couple pints of ale.

"When in the course of human events…" may have been the soberest written words in the much-beloved American document.

Then, soon after our Declaration of Independence came the signing of our Constitution. Something that, in 1777, George Washington was said to celebrate by running up a bar tab of over $17,000.

Using today's math, that's roughly an astounding $419,518.

Our country's first president clearly had a love for alcohol. Not only did he run his own whiskey distillery, but during his presidency, Washington toured the country and stayed at a different drinking tavern from town to town.

He wanted to be in touch with his countrymen as our fragile, newborn nation was taking its first baby steps into the brave new world. And what better way to connect with local communities than to visit every bar along the way.

Great writers of the day like Walt Whitman and Henry David Thoreau offered their support to the cause by portraying the barroom as a nearly utopian model of American decorum and the ultimate egalitarian meeting place.

You have to love those descriptions.

But remember, bars aren't about booze. They're about people.

Not only were taverns and pubs considered respectable in the early United States, but so were the tavern and saloon keepers that ran them.

American icon Mark Twain noted as much in his book, *Roughing It*:

> *For a time, the lawyer, the editor, the banker, the chief desperado, the chief gambler, and the saloon-keeper, occupied the same level in society, and it was the highest. The cheapest and easiest way to become an influential man and be looked up to by the community at large, was to stand behind a bar, wear a cluster-diamond pin, and sell whiskey. I am not sure but that the saloon-keeper held a shade higher rank than any other member of society.*
>
> *To be a saloon-keeper and kill a man was to be illustrious.*

These respected saloon proprietors provided the backbone of one of America's proudest institutions. And it was their sweat equity that paid for the evolution of seventeenth- and eighteenth-century taverns into saloons, grogshops, barrelhouses, hotel bars, and then eventually, the American bar.

THE EVOLUTION OF BARTENDING IN THE UNITED STATES

Award-winning drinks writer Dave Wondrich broke American bartending into three periods following the country's founding:

ARCHAIC PERIOD (1783-1830)

Taverns and pubs were widely used across the country by early Americans from most social strata, but the drinks and bar tools available were rudimentary. At this point, the term "bartender" hadn't been invented. Saloon proprietors and tavern owners were still pouring spirits but were more widely recognized as "keepers of the bar." Until something incredible came along and changed everything.

Ice!

BAROQUE PERIOD (1830-1885)

Suddenly, the keepers of the bar were no longer at the mercy of the spirit in the bottle. They could create. They could *cook* cocktails from a medley of ingredients and recipes, using ice the way a chef might a flame.

Before ice, the closest thing you might get to a cocktail was a barkeep pouring whiskey into a dirty glass. If you were lucky, he might spit in the glass once in a while to give it a nice shine.

But the availability of ice, through innovative refrigeration and transportation, turned the American bar on a dime. Frozen water pebbles, rocks, and cubes were giving the barkeep a new superpower. And a new name.

Bartenders, now equipped with the ability to create something you could sip on and enjoy.

And compared to the turpentine and moonshine we were swigging raw, it was an absolute revelation. Cocktails became floral and fresh. They were balanced, and for the first time, much more than palatable. *They were delicious.*

Imagine trading in paint thinner for piña coladas.

And though the coconut cream king wouldn't be invented until nearly a century later, a lot of classics *were.* The foundational kind. Cocktails that modern-day drinks are derived from and are still just simple deviations away from.

With ice came revelry. But it was extremely limited at first. So that revelry came at a premium. The front line for this cocktail revolution was reserved for the elite. While the day laborers were still drinking swill, celebrities and politicians were getting drunk on fancy libations. They trotted their asses into bars, in hopes of catching the diamond-studded, best-dressed man in the bar—*behind the bar*—pouring flames between mixing cups.

Crowds didn't just pay for the drinks. They paid for the show.

And they paid well.

During the Baroque period, good bartenders were considered wizards, sages, and showmen, hobnobbing with presidents, prime ministers, and royalty. The most famous of them all, Professor Jerry Thomas, was the subject of David Wondrich's book *Imbibe!*.

Jerry Thomas became an international celebrity during the middle of the nineteenth century and wrote the first cocktail book. At one point, he was making more money than the Vice President of the United States. He was known for wearing diamonds on his shirts and on every finger. And he was the one tossing whiskey, *aflame,* back and forth between tin cups.

The Blue Blazer, he called it.

A rooster of a cocktail only a ringmaster of his caliber could envision, let alone execute.

He commonly served the crooks, gold miners, politicians, and biggest prizefighters of the day. Like some of the greats to follow, Jerry Thomas died a legend. And in legendary fashion. The front page of the New York paper *The World* shared news of Thomas's passing in 1885 like this:

Apoplexy, in those days, was a diagnosis given to someone when their heart unexpectedly gave out. But it was typically reserved for describing those who'd lived a life so full their heart simply burst, having given all it could possibly give to others and to this world.

He would not be the last great bar legend to suffer this fate.

CLASSIC PERIOD (1885-1928)
Cocktails became mainstream.

Ice was widely available. Bar tools, ingredients, and recipes followed suit, resulting in cocktails making their way to the working class!

Great American writers Ernest Hemingway and F. Scott Fitzgerald honored the staples in their work, portraying visceral imagery that fans could almost taste from the page. For the first time, cocktails became part of the American lexicon and were widely available to everyone, regardless of social status.

As bars proliferated across the country, so did the profession of bartending. What was once wizardry was now a teachable craft. Master bartenders took novices under their wings, the same way an apprentice might shadow a master blacksmith until they were one day good enough to make and wield their own sword.

Bartenders passed down knowledge to their apprentices, who then passed down teachings to new apprentices of their own. Techniques, styles, but most importantly the significance of being of service to the guest. These proud apprentices were key in pushing the envelope for the craftsmanship of cocktails and service that we still enjoy today.

We have a special name for them in the business.

Barbacks.

AND THEN CAME THE TEMPERANCE MOVEMENT

It's difficult to trace when exactly the puritans began to demonize bars and alcohol. High and mighty lecturers used the Bible to weaponize their claim that drinking was bad and God would not approve of barroom behavior. Which is ironic, as *wine* is referenced 231 times, on roughly 20 percent of the pages, in the King James Version. Nonetheless, pushback was gaining steam. Right around the nineteenth century, the hostile environments of frontier saloons, New Orleans barrelhouses, and New York grogshops finally gave these teetotalers some real wings.

The Temperance Movement (the effort against legalized drinking) was the first time our country faced true anti-alcohol momentum. Bars were in serious jeopardy, and the growing culture of the time wasn't doing the business any favors.

We were getting sloppy.

Many frontier saloons had urinals and spittoons installed in the face of the bar. The issues regarding disease and sanitation back then were enough to shut the whole thing down.

But worse off, we were getting dangerous.

Shootings at saloons were common. Celebrated, in fact. It was said a good cowboy never drank past the number of bullets in his chamber. Between the booze, the gambling, and the prostitution, the young guns were hair-triggered to say the least.

These establishments, which were riddled with crime, became examples for the Temperance movement to spur up a fervor against alcohol. They used isolated events and propaganda to discredit every bar in the country.

Now, I'm all for those who might be anti-alcohol. That may prefer a zero-tolerance position when it comes to bars and booze in their own personal lives. But before we ignore the positives—*the strengths of the business*—let's keep in mind that there have been a lot of damn good people trying to keep the ship upright. And if we had all caved into the puritanical thinking of the time, turning some real shitholes into upstanding community locales would have never been possible.

Like the Golden Gopher, for example. When we broke ground, calling that area of Downtown LA the Devil's doorstep would've been a compliment! But instead of bulldozing it, we breathed life and heart back into the Gopher. And thus, into the surrounding metropolis as well.

Again, bars aren't about booze. They're about people.

The people (more specifically, the crack dealers) were the problem when I walked into the Gopher for the first time. If we had we eliminated all the bars in Downtown LA because of them, we would have killed the most thriving aspect of America's second-largest city.

However, in 1902, the book *The Saloon and Anarchy* made its way into the conversation and tied saloons straight to anarchy, providing a call to action to exorcise the demon's juice right off the face of the Earth.

A true middle finger to the bar business.

Propaganda gave life to the Temperance Movement, helping it steadily rise in popularity. And they were *good* at it. Publishing over a million pages of anti-alcohol sentiment and issuing ridiculous defamations of bars wherever and whenever they had the chance.

While there were indeed dangerous activities taking place at several saloons in the country, the vast majority of alcohol-serving bartenders and establishments continued to serve their customers graciously. As alcohol and bars made their way from saloons to mainstream society, the depiction of anarchy and lawlessness held less water.

Until 1917, when the Volstead Act, or the National Prohibition Act, passed, becoming the Eighteenth Amendment to our Constitution. This led to the largest alcohol buying binge in history. Everyone wanted to get their purchases in before Prohibition went into effect.

Prohibition officially took effect in 1920, and when it did, we did everything we could to get our hands on a drink. Including the advent of speakeasies. Speakeasies, many of which were owned by ladies, became extremely popular with women. This ushered in a new era since previously, women were not even allowed in most bars in the United States. Now, they weren't just allowed.

They were the ones in charge.

Soon, the price of alcohol skyrocketed on the black market. Against its very design, the amendment didn't curtail drinking at all, as people found all sorts of ways to obtain booze in every city. Ironically, this led to a giant wave of corruption and, ultimately, more violence than before Prohibition.

A new spike in lawlessness.

With new types of criminals. The likes of Al Capone, Machine Gun Kelly, and Bonnie and Clyde became household names.

It also destroyed a lot of jobs.

Not only did distilleries, breweries, and wineries have to close their doors, but so did all of the bar owners. Meaning all their bartenders, servers, and staff lost their jobs.

According to economists, Prohibition was an economic disaster for the United States. Before the amendment passed, a large portion of the US federal budget had been funded by the excise tax on alcohol.

As it turns out, the reason Prohibition finally ended was simple.

The government ran out of money.

President Roosevelt had the bright idea to use the taxes again from alcohol to help bail out the country from the Great Depression.

And so…

PROHIBITION ENDS

In 1933, the Twenty-First Amendment was passed, repealing the Eighteenth Amendment. Coming out of Prohibition, bars flourished. During World War I and II, they became the public's central meeting place to exchange information regarding our troops overseas by piecing together letters people received in the mail.

Some joyous. Some soul-crushing.

People cried together. Mourned together. But more than any-thing, they used bars as a place for solidarity, once again in uncertain times, to conjure strength.

MODERN TIMES

Cocktails went through a bit of a rough period between the 1950s and 1970s.

Mainly because of a surge in American commercialism. Some called it the "the McDonald's effect." Canned syrups and other cost-efficient, artificial ingredients became the norm. People were subjected to lesser-quality cocktails made for speed and convenience over substance. The imagination of the bar world dwindled.

Especially with cocaine becoming so popular.

Classic balanced cocktails and fresh ingredients were on the brink of extinction. Every martini seemed to have a fire engine red cherry in it. The kind that was bleached with calcium chloride and sulfur dioxide to better absorb the high fructose corn syrup and included a little Red #4 food coloring.

Needless to say, America was due for a cocktail renaissance.

And Dale "King Cocktail" DeGroff was just the bartender to give it to us.

The gracious writer of this book's foreword, DeGroff revived craft cocktails in the 1980s during his time at the Rainbow Room. He is revered as one of the most distinguished champions of the cocktail landscape, and he will forever be known as the guiding light responsible for course-correcting a country whose cocktail scene was lost at sea.

Dale pioneered the use of fresh ingredients in lieu of repugnant artificial mixes typical at that time. He's namely known for his unique ability to dig up classic recipes from out-of-print pre-Prohibition cocktail books and dazzle guests with their resurrection. Insisting on fresh juices and ushering in a Golden Age of cocktails, DeGroff's influence led to legendary bars like Flatiron Lounge and Milk & Honey coming to life.

Opened in 2000 by the late Sasha Petraske, Milk & Honey set a new standard for cocktail bars. Sasha's passion took the preparation of classic cocktails and service to a new level that was often copied but hard to replicate. He went on to become one of the most influential bartenders and owners of his generation, opening and reimagining bars all around the world.

Moving into the twenty-first century, there has been an explosion in good cocktail bars throughout the country (and the world). Now, solid drinks with fresh ingredients are the *standard* and can be found at bars in almost every American city.

PASSING THE TORCH

YES, you can have a career as a bartender. In fact, you can make a hell of a career for yourself. It's one of the longest-standing positions in our country, and it's survived pandemics, Civil Wars, World Wars, and even Prohibition.

Our past has not always been glorious. We've made mistakes in this country. Big ones. We've been bruised and cut and left with scars that will take generations to recover from.

If they *ever* heal.

But every single painful step of the way, bars, bar keeps, and bartenders have been there for us. They've been the shoulders the giants in our country stood upon. They've provided a place for us to lick our wounds when we fell short. And then they wiped our brow and built us back up so we might fight another day.

A place to reinforce new bonds through the clanging of mugs and the spilling of suds.

Because when America was *good*, bars were the first place we went to celebrate.

And it was the bartender doing the serving. Along with the connecting, the listening, and the healing. There's great nobility in those wearing such hats. Which is why so many people in our country's history have become damn successful in choosing it as their proud career.

When you become a bartender, you are joining a long-standing legacy of those before you who kept our bars and taverns alive in the face of some of this country's most dire times. Tavern keepers that kept the rum handy for Paul Revere and world-renowned showmen that lit whiskey on fire and tossed it between twin tins to the delight of their crowd.

The day you set foot behind a bar, you keep their spirits alive. And the longer your career, the longer they live through you.

Until one day you pass the torch, and some young apprentice keeps your legend alive.

It's this familial circle of life and death and resurrection within a bar that has made it the constant, driving force it has been for hundreds of years in America.

America started in a goddamn bar, alright. And I promise it will end there too.

CHAPTER FOUR

HOW TO GET YOUR FOOT IN THE DOOR

(At the Right Bar)

"The sole meaning of life is to serve humanity."
—Leo Tolstoy, eight-time Nobel Prize nominee

I f you aren't working in a bar yet, this chapter will help get you in. If you're already in the business but you're struggling, it'll help get you back on track.

But before we continue, let's pause for a short celebration. Here's why.

You just put a fat *win-win* card in your back pocket. If you read this chapter and follow the tools inside it, you will get the job. In any bar you like.

And if you follow these tools and *do not* get the job, well then consider yourself lucky. Because a bar that doesn't hire you after following these tips is *not* the bar you want to work for.

So, cheers to you.

WORKING AT A BAR = BEING OF SERVICE TO OTHERS

The service industry sector is by far the largest in the United States, employing almost 108 million people as of 2019. That's roughly a third of the country's population. Suffice to say, the bar business is one of the fastest-growing segments of the service sector. And it's not because of cutting-edge bar techniques and drinks.

It's because bars take care of people.

If you skipped the last chapter, being of service to each other helped our species survive global threats like famine, epidemics, and, well, *ourselves*. We must serve each other to prolong and contribute to the advancement of humanity. To be frank, in my experience, *not* being of service to others lends itself to growing a little selfish.

And selfish people generally end up alone or surrounded by other selfish people.

I agree with Tolstoy. Being of service to others is the reason we're here on Earth. If humans refused to care for each other, we'd cease to exist.

You can't be successful behind the bar if you're opposed to serving others. And furthermore, there's no *pretending*.

You can fool your mind into thinking you're giving 100 percent. But you can't fool the heart.

Now that we're clear on that, let's go get the job.

HOW TO DETERMINE THE BAR YOU SHOULD WORK AT

The first step to success as a bartender is identifying the *type* of bar you want to work at. There are more types of bars than I could possibly name, and each type is a great choice for certain people, for certain reasons. I don't know your reasons.

YOU DO.

Offhand, a few popular types of bars are: wine, sports, beer, brewpub, gay, lesbian, restaurant, cocktail, neighborhood, dive, hotel, rock 'n' roll, pub, tavern, etc. It's important to commit yourself to the type of bar you really love and can see yourself at for years to come. And then, if you like tiki bars for example, go to the most elite, badass tiki bar available, and start *there*.

Disclaimer: Be wary of nightclubs. I've never seen nightclubs as being in the same category as bars. They tend to have a much shorter lifespan. Sure, you can make a ton of money bartending at a hot nightclub, but the burnout rate is *much* higher too. It's almost purely transactional, devoid of building sustainable careers through being of service to others.

Also, you do not need to "work your way up" to a cool bar. You are cool enough as is. Plus, there will be plenty of "working your way up" in the bar of your dreams once you get there.

This chapter is about getting you to that bar. The right bar for you, where you can be of service to others and kickstart *your* incredibly rewarding career.

1. VISUALIZE YOUR FAVORITE TYPE OF BAR

Determining which type of bar you should work for is simple. Just ask yourself, "What kind of bars do I love going to? What kind of bars would I be passionate about running someday?" Your answer will help you determine the type of sacred temple of camaraderie and inebriation you should be committing your career to.

Personally, I have a passion for *neighborhood* bars. The warmer, the better. Leaning against a bar and talking to old friends or making new ones is where I'm most comfortable in the world. It's my safe place to chat with total strangers. And it's the best place for me to connect with people in any city and learn about that town from those who know it best.

The locals.

2. GET INSIDE THE HIRING MANAGER'S HEAD

So, now that you have visualized your dream bar, you're probably wondering, "How the heck do I get a job there?" At the best bars, the managers and owners are dying to hire someone who works hard, takes ownership, and loves taking care of people.

The most important thing you can do is get in the mindset of the person who will be hiring you—the general manager (GM) and/or the owner(s). You want to get inside their head in terms of what they're looking for in their staff. And trust me, they know *exactly* what they are looking for.

We know what we're looking for in our bar staff. When we find it, we pounce. We'll be all over you like bar flies on an old Galiano bottle. Our business wouldn't be anything without the hard-working people we've found who are dedicated to being of service to others.

You'll notice that so far, I haven't mentioned one word about hiring someone with prior experience.

Here's some humble pie.

Anytime I hear someone say they are a "mixologist" rather than a "bartender," a huge red flag goes up. Usually, this terminology means someone cares more about their "expert" drinks and self-promotion than being part of a hard-working, service-oriented bar *team*.

In the words of author and legendary bartender Eric Alperin:

> *I have witnessed an epidemic of bartenders jumping from one bar opening to the next because they want to be a part of the shiny new thing. This kind of behavior is rooted in a part of the ego that is detrimental to considerate and thoughtful service. You can't be present in your current line of work if you're already thinking about how to get to the next gig. Do yourself a favor, find a bar home and commit to it. This is how we all learn what it means to be a member of a bar family, and commitment goes a long way in your learning curve.*

3. BRUSH UP ON THE BAR'S RECIPES

Once you have your dream bar in mind, go to it.

We have a huge advantage in our business that many other industries simply do not have the capacity to offer. If you wanted to be an astronaut, you'd be hard-pressed to make your way past NASA onto a shuttle to check out for yourself what the vibe was like at zero gravity. But in the bar world, before you're an employee, you're allowed to be a customer just like anybody else.

Take advantage of that. Visit the bar. *Frequently.*

It may sound obvious, but you'd be surprised how many applicants have never been to the bar they're applying for. When we host interviews, we can instantly tell the person who responded to an online ad versus someone who's had one of our bars on their radar for some time. They don't have to ask about the drinks, the service style, the ambience.

They experienced it last night.

Listen to the difference in these two answers to the question, "Why did you apply here today, and how did you find out about our bar?"

Answer A: "Saw it on Craigslist."

Answer B: "I fucking LOVE this bar and would do anything to work here."

Who would *you* hire?

And speaking of ads, here's another insight. You don't have to wait for a job opening or listing to apply. Our bar group has a low turnover rate (something we are exceptionally proud of), but most bars are always looking to add someone, whether they're actually in the process of hiring or not.

Even if they *tell you* they are not hiring, you can always leave a résumé.

Or twelve.

More on résumés later.

Now, if your goal is to sling warm, cheap beer to college kids out the back door at two a.m., then learning the basics of that bar's drink menu might not be so important.

But *some bars* out there have won national awards for the cocktails they serve.

So it doesn't hurt to know a little bit about them before walking into your interview. You don't need to have them mastered—that will come much later.

On the topic of making drinks, at the end of the day, you do need to have the ability to make balanced cocktails to be considered a decent bartender. Learning how to quickly and accurately mix the most commonly ordered drinks is a necessity.

But please, do not get your head lost up some cocktail book's ass.

To be successful at a vast majority of bars, you seldom need to know how to make more than a dozen drinks. And how well you execute them comes down to one thing.

Practice.

In the words of another author and legendary bartender, Gary Regan:

Anyone can make a good drink if he puts his mind to it. It's just a case of using the best ingredients in the correct proportions and mixing them according to the prescribed method. No method of mixing a drink—apart from the hard shake, I guess—takes too long to learn or perform. What it does take, however, is becoming a speedy bartender, and anyone new at the job should know from the beginning that speed will come only with practice.

Hint: Your ability to execute to a bar's standards is expected to come over time. Whatever you do, *do not* be insecure about applying to the bar you love because you think you won't be able to hang with the giants in the room. Knowledge of the products behind the bar will follow, as will your rapport with the clientele. Any hiring manager worth their salt should realize that—and will give you time to get your sea legs under you.

They aren't hiring the bartender *you are.*

They're hiring the bartender you have the potential *to be.*

4. CREATE YOUR RÉSUMÉ

In order to be ready for your interview, you'll need to build a résumé. That word can feel like it carries a lot of weight, especially if you don't already have one. But I assure you it's nothing to be intimidated by.

As I said, bar managers and owners are constantly looking for people like you, so let's make sure that *you* come across in your résumé. While some bars don't require a formal one, I still recommend making a résumé anyway. It shows you are a professional and that you are serious about building a career.

Before listing your work and education, include a cover letter explaining how passionate you are about that bar and wanting to build your career there. This is your first chance to let the GM and/or owner know exactly what you love about their place and how much you would appreciate the opportunity to work hard and help the bar build regulars.

But it's got to be genuine. Which brings us to my next point.

Don't exaggerate.

Most people lie on their résumé. For some reason, it's considered normal.

But in our business, there's absolutely no reason to lie, mislead, or embellish. Being honest and showcasing your passion for a particular bar in your cover letter and résumé is usually enough for most bar managers and owners to want to interview you.

Lying is not confident. It's the opposite. It's insecure. A glossed-out résumé dedicated to deceit and trumped-up accomplishments is *amateur hour.*

It's also unwise.

Your first job in a bar doesn't require false accomplishments. Remember, this is a job that anyone, regardless of experience, education, social class, etc., can get. So not only is being deceitful unnecessary, but it's also something a hiring manager can smell a mile away.

And it stinks to high hell.

Don't shoot yourself in the foot before you even start. Lying at this stage of the game sets a shit precedent and is all risk and no reward.

Now let's go over how to nail that damn interview.

5. THE INTERVIEW

An important fact to know, and remember, before your interview begins is this.

The hiring manager needs hard-working, kind people more than you need the job.

It's difficult to imagine it this way, especially if you wake up the morning of the interview—like most of us do—with a few extra nerves in your gut. If you find yourself feeling a little anxious as your interview begins, congratulations.

You're human.

But again, they need you more than you need them.

Own that, and draw some healthy confidence from it as your interview begins.

Once you're in it, first and foremost, please don't try to bull-shit anyone.

You didn't lie on your résumé, so don't start now. Even if the interview's not going well. Some people come in as straight shooters with tons of potential, and then in the span of one curveball question, they flush all their real experience, personality, and passion down the drain by spitting something out that *everyone* in the room knows is a lie.

That's what you call *bombing.*

It's not too different from a first date, really. If you start panicking and fumbling all around to try to maintain that last grasp you have on the evening, you'll come off desperate. Full of shit. And not trustworthy enough for a *second* date.

Another bit of advice. Don't come in boasting about how great you are. No, I'm not talking about a first date anymore (though that applies as well). Ask yourself: what sounds better to you if *you* were the hiring manager?

POTENTIAL BAR EMPLOYEE A STARTS THE INTERVIEW:
"Hi, nice to meet you. I'm Spirit McSpiritson. I've bartended all the around the world, make the best drinks ever—probably stuff you've never heard of—I've been written about it more magazines than I can count, and I'm overqualified for the job, but if we can agree on promoting me to GM soon, I could really help your drink program—because you need it."

POTENTIAL BAR EMPLOYEE B STARTS THE INTERVIEW:
"Hi, nice to meet you. I'm Rebecca. I love this bar. I wanted to be prepared for this interview, so I came in twice this week as a customer, and I love the whiskey list. I love the vibe, and I love the clientele that you've built here. But most of all, your staff really seems to love working here too. When I came in on Monday, one of your bartenders, Jude, remembered my name, nailed my drink order, and really made me feel at home."

When serotonin rains, it pours.

Not only is Rebecca, in this example, creating instant serotonin flow in the room, but the hiring manager is also getting a firsthand look at her potential to Pour with Heart. Rebecca shows that she can recognize quality service and understands how it drives repeat business. She *gets it*. And she's made that abundantly clear to the hiring manager—while also offering a genuine compliment to the bar—before they even asked a single question.

Don't be a Spirit McSpiritson.

Despite what he might proclaim, Spirit is not the best bartender *ever*. In my mind, he doesn't have the first clue on how to Pour with Heart. If he's arrogant and condescending in the interview, then what's to change when he's in front of a guest?

If you waste your interview time bragging about drinks and awards and say nothing about being of service to customers, in my book, you've bombed. And by the way, there's no pressure to *be* the best bartender ever when you're a new hire.

You're not expected to be great yet! You're expected to work your ass off and take care of customers. Becoming great comes later.

People in the bar industry can spot a bullshitter a mile away. So, look the hiring person *straight in the eye* and convey your passion for their bar and our industry. The power of direct eye contact is amazing. It builds trust and tells the other person you have nothing to hide. It also tells them you are focused and will extend that kind of awesome eye contact with their customers.

As service guru and retail magnate Sam Walton famously preached, "Never underestimate the power of looking strangers in the eye and talking to them."

While you're looking them in the eye, do yourself a favor and *listen*. Do not take this simple step for granted. If you go in guns blazing with your own agenda and script, you're likely to miss the questions being asked of you. This is a recipe for disaster.

So is tanking the "availability" question. Every hiring manager will ask what your availability is at some point in the interview. The answer is *full availability*.

Of course, all of us have *some unavailability*, but what you're saying to the hiring manager is that you want to make their bar your number one priority, and that you're willing to rearrange your time and other priorities around it.

It's an easy way to show you *really* want to be at that bar.

Along those lines, do your best to convey that you will do *any job* there. The stuff that people like to do least? Let them know you'll do that FIRST. Managers love hearing the assurance in your voice when you convey this to them. It shows that you're humble. And *hungry*.

Any job. Any time.

As for me, personally, I love when an experienced bartender comes to us and is willing to start off as a barback. If you're willing to bust your ass at the entry level, you will earn the respect of the *entire* bar team. They will know *immediately* that you are unselfish about setting them up for success.

There's something very telling about taking an entry-level position in our business. It doesn't project weakness.

It projects strength.

And humility when you show, not just say, that there is no position beneath you.

You're letting them know that by hiring you, they will be acquiring a hard-working, selfless staffer dedicated to making their bar more successful.

And then, if they ask you at the end if you have any questions, tell them yes.

"When can I start?"

6. BE PERSISTENT

Most bars have extremely high turnover. The industry average clocks in at about 80 percent, which means that most bars lose four out of five staffers each year.

"Studies show that over 80 percent of Americans do not have their dream job. If more knew how to build organizations that inspire, we could live in a world in which that statistic was the reverse—a world in which over 80 percent of people loved their jobs. People who love going to work are more productive and more creative. They go home happier and have happier families. They treat their colleagues and clients and customers better."

—Simon Sinek, author, *Start with Why: How Great Leaders Inspire Everyone to Take Action*

Bosses love persistence. Especially when they have to replace 80 percent of their staff annually.

So if you don't get hired, don't give up.

More than likely, the only reason you didn't get the job in the first place was because they didn't have a spot available. But if you've done all the above, you can be damn sure they'll be looking for somebody just like you when they *do* need someone.

Keep checking in with them.

Being persistent shows heart.

It shows vulnerability and conviction, and assures them that you are dedicated to building a career in *their* bar, if they give you a chance.

ANDREW

Andrew Abrahamson is a prime example of someone who did everything right to get hired with our bar family. Andrew made what feels like a giant step backward to most bartenders: he took a pay cut and accepted an entry-level position just to get his foot in the door at his favorite bar on the planet.

Fortunately for us, that bar was Seven Grand, Los Angeles.

Despite years of success under his belt already and a sterling reputation for resuscitating bar programs and service models in several popular West Coast venues, Andrew showed up for work on day one with a bar towel and an apron.

As a barback.

And since 2008, he's remained a fixture with us, building a remarkable career along the way. He came in with an amazing attitude, and he showed us *immediately* that he was willing to work hard and have everyone's back.

His aptitude for service soared off the charts—behind, in front, and all around the bar. Because what Andrew did *best* was Pour with Heart.

Every. Single. Day.

Andrew advanced through the ranks of Seven Grand until he earned the position of General Manager. He led his team with steadfast devotion. He made our bar a landmark in the Downtown community, driving sales at Seven Grand higher and higher by multiplying our regulars more than we ever thought possible.

Not only did Seven Grand become the highest-grossing bar in our company, but in all of Los Angeles as well.

In 2019, Andrew took over as COO of our company. From ringing out mop heads to becoming *the head* of operations for our entire family of bars nationwide.

And it all started with Andrew picking his dream bar. Going to his dream bar. Then being persistent enough to get his foot in the door at his dream bar. And when he got his interview, he made sure—if he conveyed *just one thing*—it was that he was going to work his ass off in order to help our bar succeed.

He laid his dedication on the table, and our bar family will forever be grateful for it.

As special as Andrew is, his approach is something you can mirror. Along with his career path. And when you do, like Andrew, the sky is the *fucking* limit.

CHAPTER FIVE

*DISCLAIMER ONE THE WRONG BAR CAN BE A CAREER KILLER

"A family is a place where minds come in contact with one another. If these minds love one another, the home will be as beautiful as a flower garden. But if these minds get out of harmony with one another, it is like a storm that plays havoc with the garden."
—The Buddha

Culture and intention.

Two words that run through the bar industry like vapor.

The problem with them? They're intangible.

You can't touch culture.

You can't hold intention in the palm of your hand.

And worst of all, their interpretation varies from venue to venue. Which can make them difficult to course-correct when a bar finds itself running off the tracks.

Assuming it started on the tracks to begin with.

But before we can dissect the good from the bad, we need to delve into what culture and intention mean behind the bar.

Culture in this business starts with the shared values of the bar team.

Everyone has their own personal value system. But the values we believe in aren't relegated to us alone. A lot of people view things in a similar fashion. From their overall outlook on the world to the way they believe people should be treated.

When we find people in our personal lives who share our values, we tend to gravitate toward them. Often this leads to friendships, and even life partners and soulmates. When we run into those whose values conflict with ours, we tend to avoid them at all costs.

Unfortunately, inside the tight-quartered meat grinder that is a bar on any busy night, there's no such thing as avoiding those with different values.

It doesn't take a staff of twenty to be misaligned either. It can be two bartenders on two different pages, and I'll tell you what that shift's going to be like.

Hell.

For everyone. For *both* bartenders. For the staff. For every customer who makes the mistake of walking in that night.

A bar staff can't be completely of service to their customers when they're distracted by their own in-house bullshit. Which is why guests can *feel* when a bar's culture is a downer.

But guests can also feel when a bar's culture is rocking.

When it's obvious the staff enjoys working together. That they stick up for each other, rally for each other, take pride in getting out of bed in the morning (or afternoon) for each other. They have more resilience during the down times. And more gratitude when celebrating the good.

In other words, they bleed together. And they succeed together. It's those shared values they have in common, the strength of their culture, that *keeps them together.*

When the shared values of the staff are aligned, the bar shines and the guest wins.

If you don't share the same values as your bar team, it's time to look for another team.

Consider these two questions:

Does the bar staff you work with (or are considering working with) share the same values with each other? And secondly, do you share the same values of that bar's culture?

In our bar family, rather than crossing our fingers that we were all on the same page regarding our culture, we decided to articulate our values out loud. We did this by having everyone in our bar family vote on the values they found most important. From that list, we adopted the six most popular. Now, over a hundred members of our bar family identify so strongly with those shared values that they have symbols of them tattooed on their skin.

This is not to say tattooing symbols to represent your bar's values is right for everyone, but it does show a rare commitment to culture that we are damn proud of.

At the time of writing this book, I have four of these tattoos, and I'm running out of real estate for my fifth and sixth. I think the inside of my forearm might be the next spot, so every time I roll up my sleeves, I'm reminded.

Once you have a good idea about a bar's culture, the next thing you'll want to examine is their intention.

A successful bar is all about setting the right intention.

In our bar family, for example, it is our intention to take care of each other. We attempt to do this in every bar, with everybody. That means being completely of service to our customers, our community, and every last brother and sister we have on staff.

In the end, it's our shared values that keep our intentions grounded. Keep them pure. Intention and culture should complement one another that way.

The left hand washing the right kind of thing.

If a bar's intention is not to take care of people, then really, what the fuck are they even doing? That bar will struggle at building repeat business, which will translate to fewer opportunities for someone like you while working there.

The definition of a true dead-end job.

But that's not what this book is about. I want you to be a badass with unlimited upside.

So don't work in a shitty bar culture. And don't work under assholes with bad intentions.

HOW THE BAR INDUSTRY SAVED ME

I needed redemption after a career in the financial world. Reduced to studying data on computer screens all day, I was sorely disconnected from humanity.

My escape was bars.

I spent almost every night closing them down, which was brutal since I had to be up so damn early the next morning. Bars always had such a strong hold on me.

A place that felt like home.

So, when I entered the bar world professionally, I vowed that I would return the favor. That intention led me to discover a rich subculture of creative, hard-working people I wanted to support and who also supported me.

I'm so fucking lucky to have found my calling.

But along the way, here's something that *I did*, that you can also do, that worked wonders.

From the beginning, I made a conscious decision not to work for assholes. You can (and should) make the same choice, because that's what it really is. A choice.

And for the sake of this chapter, that choice begins well before you find yourself working for these assholes. It begins with the bar you decide to work at. I don't care if a bar is the coolest in town or if it's got the best press in America. Don't work there if the intentions of the ownership and/or management come from a bad place.

You know when it ain't right. And you have *every right* to get up and walk away.

Professionally.

Just because someone accepts your application, interviews you, and even offers you employment, you do not have to accept.

It's important you understand this. If you sense there is something rotten in Denmark during your hire, trust me, it's not going to change or get better over time.

You'll regret it every day.

If you work at the wrong bar and for the wrong people, you might find yourself becoming disheartened and missing out on the real magic available to you as a bartender.

I don't want that for you.

I want you to work with humble people who love and respect each other. Even if the bar's not "cool," working there will be a blast, and you will celebrate its success *together* like champions.

THREE CLUES YOU'RE WORKING AT THE WRONG BAR

1.   THE BAR IS A CONCEPT YOU LOVE BUT DON'T RESPECT

It's important to be honest with yourself and work for the type of bar you love. If your heart skips more of a beat for tiki bars than it does for dives, go sell some rum. But before you join any bar team, ask yourself a deeper question.

Do you respect the bar...within the bar concept?

For example, if you love sports bars, do you think the sports bar you're aiming to get hired at is doing it right? Because being in love with a bar concept alone is not a reliable enough gauge of your future success. If that sports bar is shady with money, awful to guests, and worse to staff, then the fact that they have the game on during your shift won't be enough for you to put your heart and soul into working there.

If you love the concept but don't respect the bar, then it's best to go elsewhere.

2. THE SERVICE SUCKS

For too many bars, quality service never gets out of the gate. This is almost always a result of setting forth the wrong intention with that bar to begin with.

For example, if someone opens a bar for the wrong reason— say, only to make money, get laid, or get hammered—then the staff will take on the same mindset and the service will inherently suffer. Greed and lust will push management away from focusing on taking care of their bar staff and patrons.

If you take the low road, you're going to end up in the ditch.

How the hell are you ever going to build a career from there? If management is in it for the wrong reasons, don't expect a fair shot at success. Their tunnel vision will blind them from recognizing your achievements and talent.

They won't reward you for Pouring with Heart.

Instead, they'll likely promote others for backstabbing and betraying your team to get ahead.

3. THE BOSS

Businessinsider.com reported on a recent study that revealed that one in five CEOs display "psychopathic traits." That's 20 percent. That's also the same rate found in the average prison population.

Sometimes we think we have an obligation to our superior, regardless of their behavior.

Their integrity. Their quality of basic human character.

In the blue-collar world, there's a lunch pail attitude that you clock in, clock out, and don't make too much of a fuss in between.

Asshole bosses thrive on this.

It sheds them of accountability and moral decency. You can easily spot them by how condescending they are. How they talk down to their team and customers, often refusing to look them in the eye. They prey on the fact that their employees feel obligated to serve under them just because they are the boss.

Fuck that. Find a better boss.

Your "superior" is flesh and blood, just like you. They're not better than you. They don't deserve absolute loyalty despite their actions. They need to earn it like everyone else.

If you ever find yourself in a position where you think you have to stick it out and "be a good soldier," you're setting yourself up for wasting your talent, your time, and your potential career.

Find a boss who takes pride in being good to their people.

WHAT DO I DO IF I'M AT THE WRONG BAR?

So, if you decide you are at the wrong bar, how do you handle it?

Here's a hard truth.

There isn't much you can do to change things at that bar without being in charge.

Clean up your résumé, start searching for the right bar, and move on.

You are a professional pushing for a career in this business. So now is the time to act like it, and work for (and with) other professionals. But please remember to always leave an employer the right way.

You don't need people talking shit about you in this industry.

It's a small community, and everyone knows everyone. Even more reason to set the tone of being a professional and thus gaining the reputation that comes along with being one.

YOU CAN'T "FIX" A BAR WITHOUT THE RIGHT PEOPLE

Throughout my career, I have seen many award-winning bars close their doors.

They're easy to spot the moment I walk in, despite their favorable press and accolades. Their drinks or their design may be stellar, but if the bar team is disconnected from one another and acting too good for their customers, it's only a matter of time.

A bad culture is like a cancer. There is no quick fix. Despite what the show *Bar Rescue* tries to tell you. With all due respect, that show is total bullshit.

Bar Rescue doesn't focus on the real factor that actually makes bars successful—the bar team Pouring with Heart. The host of that show is patronizing and abrasive when speaking to the staff. Much to the delight of the producers, I'm sure.

Humiliation doesn't motivate bar people. *Or any people.* It creates the exact opposite of the nurturing and trusting environment you need for a team to Pour with Heart.

In this book's introduction, I spoke about the bar that changed everything for me.

The Golden Gopher.

It's an example of a *real* bar rescue we pulled off. This is how we turned that total shithole into a game-changing success.

THE GOLDEN GOPHER *WAS* THE WRONG BAR

Opened in 1905, the Golden Gopher is the oldest operating bar in Los Angeles. It took nearly a century for it to fall into the wrong hands, but when it did, the Gopher went straight to hell. Owners with rotten intentions produced a loathsome culture that my good friend (and partner at the time) Marc Smith and I walked right into in 2002.

Because the whole operation was a front for drug dealing and prostitution, they had no real bar sales to review when it came time to purchase. Besides the rich history, there was little good about the Golden Gopher left. Still, we took a shot. And over the next six months, we tried our best to restore it with love with our designer pal, Ricki Kline.

"We rip off part of the roof," he said.

Uh…what?

Did this fucking guy just say he wanted us to bring a demolition crane onto 8th Street and chew a section of the roof out?

"Our clientele may want to smoke cigarettes while enjoying their drinks. We cannot let them do so outside. The neighborhood is too dangerous."

Ricki was right.

So we ripped that son of a bitch right off.

Twenty percent of the roof so that we could better protect our guests and make them feel safe to socialize and sometimes, as Ricki said, smoke when they drank.

We hired from within the community. Character-filled men and women who stuck together and looked out for each other. Even when the 18th Street gang was perennially trying to break into our building.

We didn't realize it at the time, but the conditions stacked against us actually united us. Most of the people from our original crew work are still with us today. And we still call ourselves *family*. As far as the loyal regulars we've built at the Gopher, many of them still call it their home. And not their second home.

Just "home."

Those regulars love our culture. And they respect our intention.

They became one with the bar and our staff, racing to tell their friends about us, building more regulars who, in turn, shared the Gopher with their circle of friends, and so on.

The Golden Gopher crawled out of the depths of despair to become a runaway success. Today, the bar is busier than ever, and its bartending positions are some of the most coveted in the city. It's a landmark of burgeoning Downtown Los Angeles and has been honored by our city's mayor for being a shining beacon of light within the community.

But still, for us, our biggest point of pride will always lay in the fact that we accomplished what we did because we were there for each other. All of us.

Transforming the Golden Gopher helped cement the direction of my life. And it's all due to the fact we created such a bond with our crew and our community.

It made us feel that nothing could fucking stop us.

Not even a global pandemic.

GOLDEN GOPHER COCKTAIL RECIPE

Here is the recipe I wrote up for the Golden Gopher Cocktail in 2004. The *Los Angeles Times* actually printed it in their newspaper for us on opening night. While I've given some delicious sources for cocktail recipe books in the Appendix, this is the only recipe you will find in *this* book:

Ingredients:

- 1 crack-infested, rundown building with a rare liquor license
- $500,000 cash investment
- 3 crazy owners wanting to open in a neighborhood of drug dealers and pimps
- 1 insane designer wanting to rip the roof from 20 percent of the building
- 1 badass bar staff
- 90 cases of booze

Directions:

1. Mix the crazy owners, the insane designer, and the badass bar staff together.

2. Rip out most of the eastern wall of the building and part of the roof.

3. Build an interior inspired by beaten-up British flats, acid flashbacks, and Liberace.

4. Add in the booze and serve.

Tip: Best served with ear-splitting rock 'n' roll.

THE RIGHT BAR

Bars are some of the most gorgeous places on Earth. From the maple-swirled bar tops to the sharpness of the stainless steel bar tools to the sultry lighting forgiving every blemish in between. But as much as aesthetics and atmosphere can take your breath away, what really constitutes the beauty of bars will always come down to one element.

The human element.

For example, the best part of a drink menu isn't the cocktails on the list. It's watching a guest's eyes light up when they look through it with a friend. The conversation that starts between them and the bartender when they find something familiar and special on that list. Or even better, when a bartender takes a guest's hand and assures their safety through a fresh and unique experience should they decide to try something new.

The best thing bars do is bring people together.

Beyond the drinks they serve, bars offer kindling for their community. Opportunity for connection and, often, reconciliation. When you work at a bar, you are more than someone who pours booze.

You are a facilitator of the human spirit.

An energy that is freely accepted and invited into your bar, coming alive under your guidance and specific care each and every shift. You are the great conductor of that energy. Which means your *work* isn't like any other kind of work.

And a bar job isn't just like any other job either.

Because of this, you owe it to yourself to question whether or not the bar you are at is the *right* bar.

Is it a bar you can put your heart and soul into? Is it a bar that is run with respect? That will encourage you to rise in character?

Or sink to a lesser version of yourself?

It takes charisma, empathy, and patience to care for people. The wrong bar will extinguish all three.

I've seen burned-out bartenders with the heart sucked out of their pours. They grow miserable, fast, and we're *all* the worse for it.

They start to pour with angst and regret and, eventually, resentment.

Resentment for the people they're supposed to be taking care of, triggered by the sound of the bell each time another customer walks in the door.

Bartending is a people business.

It's often hard to tell where the guest ends and the bartender begins. And so, what's special about people is also true of what's special about bars. They're symbiotic.

And they're all incredibly different.

Just like people, each bar has its own culture, its own personality, and its own soul.

Find the bar that best matches yours.

CHAPTER SIX

BARBACK

(The Most Important Position in the Bar)

"The journey of a thousand miles begins with a single step."
–Japanese proverb

Most careers in the bar business begin with learning how to be a great barback. This chapter will illuminate how Pouring with Heart from the ground up can help you do that.

This is as important a chapter as any in this book—for one reason.

No other industry out there lives or dies by the actions of the entry-level position. Think about it. What other business out there gives the keys to the Ferrari to a sixteen-year-old the day after they get their permit?

Barbacks start by being given keys to buildings, tools for the bar's physical operations, and access to liquor rooms full of thousands of dollars of inventory.

A mountain of trust and responsibility.

And that's on day one.

Not only that, but as a barback, the resident bartenders on staff are counting on you, NOW.

Not in a couple weeks after you get comfortable. Not after you pass your ninety-day trial. They need you to execute on your word. The promises you made to land the job in the first place.

And they need you to do it before the beer taps blow another CO_2 can. The fistfight brewing in line gets out of hand. And the wash line on the regular's drink hits the bottom of the glass.

Seriously, the seed to a great bar career starts with the most important position in the bar.

The barback.

For most, the journey to becoming successful as a bartender starts with an apron and a prayer. A lot is asked of these brave souls. But before you let the magnitude of the position scare you off, take solace in knowing it's the exact place that so many other legendary bartenders started before you. *They figured it out.*

And so will you.

If you happen to be reading this *after* graduating from the position—or having skipped it altogether—trust me, it's never too late to get back in touch with some kickass fundamentals.

No matter how great the racehorse, what makes or breaks the photo-finish always comes down to the little things.

Assuming you crushed Chapters 4 and 5 of this book, you've made it. You've gotten the job, and more importantly, you've gotten the job at a bar you love and respect. Now, you need to earn your keep by showing your new bar family you deserve to be there.

It's time to put your money where your mouth is.

BARBACKING DEFINED

You can tell from a mile away if someone has never been punched in the face before.

The same can be said about a bartender, bar owner, or general manager who's never been a barback. Who's never paid the dues that come with the bar's most primordial position.

The labor. The humility. The selflessness.

The grunt force trauma of working the hardest in the bar while being paid the least.

If you've never been behind the curtain, mucked around the underbelly of a bar, how could you ever appreciate it when the lights go up?

The job of a barback...is difficult.

And that's sugarcoating it.

But the greats wouldn't have it any other way. Because they know that barbacking in a place you love and respect signs you up for a prerequisite to Pouring with Heart.

Because if you're not learning the benefits of being completely of service to others at this entry-level position, chances are you'll never learn it. You'll never see the upside the intangibles provide that ultimately power you through the intense rigors of the job.

The barback is a first-in, last-out, carry-the-flag-into-battle-type job grounded by a code of humility and honor. They face the most insane challenges in any given bar, on every given night.

And because they're not ones to gloat about their contributions, allow me to gush.

The tightest definition for the role is this.

A barback is the person in charge of making sure the bartenders are successful at serving others. They are the bartender's apprentice, studying to become an expert bartender themselves, in time.

Usually, they're responsible for stocking the liquor, glassware, and beer, prepping the garnishes, juicing the fruit, filling ice bins, and readying the bar stations for service. Other times, they're bussing tables, dishwashing, cleaning spills, toilets, and shattered glass, hauling kegs, and breaking down bartenders' wells at the end of the night.

I've seen a barback take a punch from a drunken guest. Then get right back to work, taking out the trash and taking on drink orders for a busy bartender. Without blinking a black eye.

Because if they go down, the bar goes down.

They may be the first rung on the ladder, but without question, the performance of the barback can either fuel the engine that drives a kickass night—or—be the anchor that strands the ship, starves the crew, and conjures mutiny as piss-drunk sailors set the rum aflame before abandoning ship to Davy Jones's locker.

In short, barbacks are the backbone. The foundation. The all-encompassing support.

HARD WORK + GRIT
I get it.

Moving mountains of ice, full kegs, and endless glassware and doing all kinds of other shit work for bartenders who make much more money than you in tips can suck.

Being a barback is brutal, back-breaking, nonstop labor.

But it's also the best possible proving ground for showing your dedication to the bar, how hard you will work, and how selfless you can be.

Inside the challenges that come with the job lies an opportunity.

The top bartenders in the business always look back at their time as a barback with fondness. With great pride and gratitude. Because they know how critical their time as a barback was in shaping their career as a bartender.

It's like the minor leagues. And though some might shit on the minors, remember that's where the talent comes from. The other thing about the minors to keep in perspective is this.

You can get called up at any time.

Do not lose the perspective of time in this business. The brevity of life in a bar is unlike most industries out there. Positions can open in the blink of an eye, sometimes mid-shift.

And that hole always gets plugged first by the baddest of the barbacks.

If your bar staff is lucky enough to have one, let me tell you, *everyone* behind the bar knows who it is. Though it may not seem like it, believe me, people are paying attention. And when the shit hits the fan, if you've established yourself as a rock, they will come calling.

Not only the leaders in the organization but also the bartenders you've been supporting throughout your shift. There is a big difference between a bartender who shows up for their shift and says "phew" versus "fuck" when they see your name assigned to their well.

Without great barbacks, our bartenders aren't positioned to Pour with Heart. To be there 100 percent, the way they need to be for their customers.

A great barback is indispensable like that.

So, take pleasure in the pain. Enjoy the grind!

As you do, you'll earn the respect and trust of everyone on your team, creating war stories as your career continues down your desired path.

Not to compare this to *actual* war stories by any means, but in terms of the bar world, a great barback always has the best tales.

No matter where your career path takes you, you are going to look back and laugh about these moments of calamity. And when the bottle comes off the shelf and it's shoot-the-shit, let-your-hair-down time, you won't be the one in the room without a story.

That, I can promise.

BEING OF SERVICE

Putting your heart and soul into being of service to those around you is special for a barback.

When you're riding shotgun next to a bartender that's Pouring with Heart, you're getting a firsthand look at the magic that's occurring between them and the guest in front of you both. You can feel the serotonin by proxy, picking up on some of it for yourself.

If you're paying attention, you have a front-row seat to a great bartender who's using their magic to connect with their customers. To make them feel seen. Acknowledged. To let them know they matter.

But this beautiful interaction doesn't happen without you, the barback, setting the stage.

Doing so helps remove the potential landmines, roadblocks, and distractions that can interrupt a bartender from fully Pouring with Heart.

Watching this scenario play out can be painful with a lackluster barback at hand.

Bartender to guest: *"Welcome to our bar tonight. It's cold outside; you look like you're freezing! Let me fix you a cocktail to warm you right up. Can I suggest an Irish Coffee to start you off?"*

Barback to bartender: *"We're out of coffee."*

Guest shivers.

Bartender to guest: *"Sorry about the Irish Coffee. My mistake. But how about, instead, I fire you up a Hot Toddy to get you right?"*

Barback: *"The hot water dispenser's busted."*

Guest: *"Never mind. I'll just have a Maker's, neat."*

Barback: *"Oh, shoot. We're out of stock. But I think there might be a case in the liquor room."*

Talk about a disaster. And a wasted opportunity ripe for Pouring with Heart.

The bartender may have done everything right in this scenario—being attentive, present, and empathetic to their guest's needs—but without the support of the barback and the tools they're responsible for providing, the bartender is *fucked*.

The magic is gone, and they've let their guest down. With little to no chance that customer ever comes back to the bar. As a barback, if you're not being of service to your bartender, you are sabotaging the guest's experience and hanging your bartender out to dry.

There is nothing like a barback that tackles a problem before having to be asked to do so. Great barbacks eat, breathe, and sleep anticipating their bartender's needs.

Being of service, despite the hard work it takes, will lead you to success in this industry. How much success? Suffice to say, most of my top brass started as barbacks.

Here is a quote from Andrew Abrahamson, who, as you'll remember from previous chapters, started as a barback with us and now oversees all our operations:

We only ask two things of our barbacks—you've got to know how to hustle, and you've got to be a decent human being. If you can bring those two things to the table, we can teach you everything else. You can't undervalue the hustle, and you can't undervalue the heart. They go hand in hand. You can't have one without the other. If you have the biggest heart in the bar, but you're lazy and you sit around and watch other people work, then you're not going to make it. But also, if you're the fastest, hardest worker, but you're a prick, then it's not going to work either.

FIVE SMALL THINGS THAT MAKE
A BIG (BARBACK) DIFFERENCE

The role of the barback is the most versatile in the bar. Responsibilities change like the wind—sometimes shift to shift, sometimes hour to hour. Focusing on doing your job, and doing it well, is a good place to start. But in this game, you have to be prepared for the curveball. Expect the unexpected so when it shows up, you're not overwhelmed.

Instead, you're prepared.

Now, I couldn't possibly write down every curveball I've seen in the last twenty-five years. But what I can do is offer you five tips you can use to strengthen your toolkit so you are better prepared for anything…when *anything* strikes.

1. ESTABLISH YOUR DEPENDABILITY
Ninety percent of life is just showing up.

There are a ton of flakes in the bar industry (and almost every industry, really). So establishing yourself as dependable gets you off to a premiere start in our business. Simply making your shifts on time and being ready to work hard will help you stand out.

Now, you'll have to be disciplined. Showing up four out of five shifts on time doesn't cut it. You'll need to rid yourself of the crutch of making excuses about traffic. Yeah, traffic sucks. But it almost *always* sucks. It is not an excuse to be late. Traffic is a reason to be early.

Getting a good night's rest, getting your mind right, and then getting out your door early sets the tone for your success as a professional. Arriving early and eager to work indicates you're there with *purpose*.

That will ingratiate you with your entire team.

It's amazing how many people blow it by being late or skipping work. Not showing up on time is unprofessional. Not showing up at all is downright disrespectful and will end your career before it gets started.

2. HAVE THICK SKIN

As awesome as barbacking is, one thing it is *not* is sunshine and rainbows. On the contrary, this job is going to kick you in the teeth.

Be ready for it.

And when it does, shake it off. Learn from your mistakes, and show the kind of mettle it takes to get back up on that horse again.

At some point, the bar is going to collapse in on you during a busy night. People are going to be shouting at you—both customers *and* bartenders. It's going to be loud, raucous, and stressful to say the least. You're going to be tired, sweaty, and possibly bleeding.

But you're going to get through it.

Did I mention you were going to sweat? It's remarkable how much hard work you can wring out from a pair of socks after a hard-fought shift.

You're also going to screw up. Especially early on. There is no train wreck quite like the first night of a barback who is in way over their head. It's like a car accident on the side of the road. As bad as you feel, there's nothing you can do but watch as a new barback mixes up the wrong syrups, screws up the taps system, shuts the beer lines down, or stumbles out of the wash area and shatters an entire twenty-four-piece rack of glassware.

It's important to know we've all been there. And the sign of a successful barback is *not* whether you have these kinds of nights or not. It's what kind of character you show *after.*

Do you give up on yourself?

Or do you keep punching?

Bad moments don't define your failure. But how you bounce back from them can define your success. Whether or not you can learn from your mistakes. Or let one mistake turn into ten…which then turns into twenty, and now everyone's fucked.

Hearing the words "You are killing it" echoed down the bar line sounds a hell of a lot better than "You are killing US!"

Trust me. No matter the waters, you can right the ship.

Keep showing up.

No matter how bad a barback's first night, there is nothing like the sound of the slow clap they get when that barback— humbled and beat to shit—shows up for work the next day.

On time. With purpose. And ready to get better.

If that doesn't fire up a bar staff, nothing will.

3. TAKE RESPONSIBILITY
Remember, everyone has fucked up before.

A good bar team will teach you how to fuck up less.

Because they care about you. You're part of the family now. Which means no one is rooting for you to fail. Family picks each other up when we fall, right?

It's called taking responsibility.

Your team has your back. One of the easiest ways to fracture that is to skirt responsibility yourself. To blame others. Make excuses. Refuse to take accountability.

Remember, this is a "fail first" kind of business. Management isn't sitting back wondering whether or not a barback is ever gonna screw up. It's written in the fucking stars. So, when you don't take responsibility, it stands out like those sweaty socks at the end of the night. It's a bad look, and it lets people know that you may not be the team player the bar needs to succeed.

But if you *do* take responsibility—you show up on time/early and you look your team in the eye ready to fight another day—you will earn yourself another shift, another week.

Another month to learn from a whole new set of fuck-ups at that bar.

4. EYE CONTACT, EYE CONTACT, EYE CONTACT

By now, you know how important connection is when being of service to your team and the guests in the bar. But before you ascend to the rank of bartender, you'll want to get a head start on how to establish deeper connections.

Ways to generate the kind of impactful bonds you've witnessed bartenders form with their guests when they're Pouring with Heart.

The most basic and best way to start doing that is through eye contact.

Eye contact conveys three things essential for building strong connections with others and, ultimately, your success behind the bar: empathy, trust, and vulnerability.

We all know how frustrating it is to talk to someone who doesn't have the courtesy to look us in the eyes. It makes us feel as if we don't matter. Like we're not worth the words coming out of their mouth.

On the contrary, when someone speaks to us—and looks us in the eye—our chests puff up. Our confidence inflates, and we, for reasons we often can't pinpoint in the moment, become much more receptive to their message.

Brilliant restaurateur Danny Meyer said this about perfect hospitality in his book, *Setting the Table: The Transforming Power of Hospitality in Business*: "The first time we enter the world, we receive the purest hospitality we will ever receive with four gifts: eye contact, a smile, a hug, and some food."

Lack of eye contact has also been proven to be bad for your health. Research shows that babies develop neurological problems without enough eye contact. Likewise, adults can develop psychological disorders without a sufficient amount of eye-to-eye.

We all need eye contact. Which makes it a powerful resource for you, if you don't overlook it. It takes zero effort to look someone in the eye when you speak or listen to them.

Sometimes we have to force ourselves to do it until it becomes second nature. But it's worth it. Maintaining eye contact may *feel* uncomfortable at first, but dedicating yourself to practicing this allows you to share something special with the person you're connecting with.

The gift of being *present.*

5. DEVELOP A RAPPORT WITH YOUR BARTENDER

The barback/bartender relationship is the most sacred partnership there is in a bar. It requires tremendous chemistry, which in itself calls for patience, work, and most of all, trust.

Barbacks and bartenders have to have each other's backs. It's the only way to keep the walls from closing in on them when a spirited crowd comes to life. However, even though they practically work on top of each other, oftentimes the demands of the job don't afford a barback the time, or the opportunity, to stop and actually get to know their bartender.

Most nights, when a barback and bartender are running on all cylinders, they'll go an entire shift without *actually* even seeing each other.

And with the right kind of chemistry built between them, they won't need to.

A great tandem behind the bar can do it blindfolded. Mentally, they can finish each other's thoughts, sentences, and even drink orders. They have confidence in one another. They anticipate each other's moves and rely on that anticipation to stoke their efficiency.

Efficiency is paramount because the more time you save behind the bar, the more you can spend it where it belongs.

On the customer.

A bartender can't Pour with Heart—see their guest, hear them, connect with them—if the two of you are bumbling into each other all night like a couple of greased monkeys trying to fuck a football. If you're constantly burning wells because of broken glass. If the tins are soiled, the fruit is out, and a drink order can't be communicated between the two of you to save your lives, your customers are getting ripped off.

You and your bartender are cheapening their experience.

So, how do you find that rhythm?

Well, every bartender has a certain beat to their drum. As a great barback, make it *your* job to recognize it. Tap into it. Pay attention to their style, strengths, and tendencies. And when the two of you start bobbing your head to the same bass line, you'll understand there's a colossal difference between doing your job correctly and doing your job at the *correct time*.

Your rhythm is everything in this business. Too slow is bad, and too fast is fatal. The sooner you learn to dance with one another, the better (and quicker) your rapport will build.

Two left feet and all.

Before you know it, you'll be swimming in and out of each other's space as if the two of you were one. In no time, you'll be killing it inside your six-by-ten-foot bar area, turning that sixty square feet into the most popular, and lucrative, in the city.

And just like a dance, you'll make building regulars look easy.

When guests see you and your bartender in control of your domain, they know right away that their night is safe in your hands. And safety...is sexy. It makes us feel like we can drop our defenses and let our hair down for a couple hours. That we can sit back and trust those same bar hands—all banged up, nicked, and in a constant swollen state—to go to work.

Customers find themselves attracted to and engaged by people who *really* get along. Charmed, even.

Because we all *want that*.

A taste of that chemistry, that connection, that serotonin. No substance can match the energy a great barback and bartender can pump into a room when they're in the zone.

When they're Pouring with Heart, *together*.

Doing so creates a special bond. It's the reason why, at the end of the night, the bartender is always the first to go up to their barback and congratulate them with a stack of tips or a shot of whiskey—*or both*—and say thank you.

And often it's in that moment—both soaked in sweat and covered in booze, with a pocket full of phone numbers each—that the two finally get a chance to look each other in the eyes.

And *cheers* one another in victory.

AN INTERVIEW WITH PEDRO SHANAHAN (THE WORLD'S GREATEST BARBACK)

To fully understand the role of the barback, I wanted to include this interview with a man who truly represents the nobility of the craft. Pedro Shanahan. Who, in my opinion, is the world's greatest barback.

I do not say that lightly.

Pedro sowed his oats at Downtown LA's Seven Grand whiskey bar. He helped us break ground there, and over a decade later, he has continued to inspire those around him to be better barbacks. Better bartenders.

And better people.

Pedro remains a barback on our team *by choice*. He could have moved up to bartender or potentially even a leadership position in our bar group. But he's chosen his path.

It is rare, but some people relish the barback position so much that they want to make a career out of it. And no one's done it better than "Shananigans."

Pedro is writing his own book, aptly titled *Barback*, about the spiritual journey toward his own success. He travels the world tasting spirits and judging some of the world's finest spirit competitions. He hosts multiple spirit tastings at our venues, has run our Los Angeles health and wellness programs, sells more fancy bottles of whiskey than anyone from here to Scotland, *and* manages to run a successful podcast.

But, most importantly, Pedro takes tremendous pride in being a barback. Before working at Seven Grand, he tended bar for celebrities in Hollywood. But he got burnt out. Pedro needed a fresh start, to reset from the ground up. And so, he earned the position of barback with us and has remained at that position for over a decade. His growth within the role, however, has been nothing short of extraordinary. Pedro's got international clout from Cuba to Japan, Kentucky to Orkney, and every distillery in between. And no matter where you end up in the world, he's the kind of guy you want in your corner.

CM: *I know you love taking care of people. Where does that come from, Pedro?*

Pedro: Well, thank you. I'm humbled by that. If you really put your heart into what you do, life rewards you. You get paid back in *kind*—the more you give, the more you have. And it brings customers back because everybody wants that feeling.

One of our underlying mantras as a barback in our bar is "make shit better." And guess what? The dishes are never done, so it's a constant reminder that you must have constant effort, constant upkeep, to keep making things better, little by little.

We can't ever solve it, but we can make it better. Time and time and time again.

CM: *Why did you want to go back to a barback position and stick with it?*

Pedro: The barback always has everyone's back; they are the base support. The bartenders are creating special moments with customers, but the barback's taking care of the whole bar. Essentially, a bar runs on the backs of the barbacks. They're making sure that every piece of the action is moving in the right direction, that all the different cogs are turning. If something is going wrong, whether it's a pump underneath the bar or the beer lines acting up and the taps aren't pouring correctly, the barback is the unseen hand that makes all things all better.

There's a spiritual aspect in that as well. The idea that there doesn't need to be a face on what gets fixed, it just needs to *be* fixed. It's a selfless act.

People often think: *Oh, you're just a barback.* They think of that as being some kind of a lowbrow choice in life, like somehow, I failed. But in my mind, it's the exact opposite. I've got such a rich life. I see other people walking around, and they're bummed. They've got their briefcase and their suit, and their shoulders are hunched, and they're looking down. They don't have a life worth living. They've given up their soul for some kind of stability or some kind of imagined reward that they're going to be too tired to enjoy by the time they get there. I have tried to stay really humble and enjoy every moment I have so that I'll never be in that position. I haven't traded anything. I get the payback every single day, and that comes from caretaking. For me, the love comes from the caretaking.

What I've gotten from being a barback is a feeling of being the ultimate support for those around me.

CM: *You have had tremendous growth in the industry, but you didn't take the typical approach into leadership roles. Why is that?*

Pedro: I think my growth has been a deepening and not necessarily an ascension. I didn't necessarily move up the ladder, but I did move out from the ladder in all directions. I kind of deepened the whole idea of barbacking by making it more about education, and now, about wellness. If you have each other's backs, what does that mean? What does that look like? I think that it's about offering resources so that you could truly have a better life in the bar business. You know, there's a lot of perils in the bar business. There are drugs around. You're drinking more than the average person, perhaps. Or you have kind of hard hours a lot of times, and maybe you don't get enough sleep. Maybe you don't eat well. If we're going to create all these bars, how can we best take care of our people? How can we continue to have their backs? To have the best staff working for us, we need to really show them we care enough to want to be concerned for their physical health, their mental health, and their overall wellness.

***

I felt every minute of Pedro's interview. As much as I may have alluded to the spiritual journey of a barback earlier, Pedro's avowal says it all.

The road of unselfishness and learning how to really bust your ass starts at the barback position. A great barback prides themselves in leaving no stone unturned. That means no bartender or guest unattended. And no problem unapproached.

Barbacks are selfless. Hard-working. And dogged loyalists. They get their asses handed to them. But they keep on showing up. No matter what kind of shitshow a Friday night turns into. If there is *one* person in the bar you can count on to see things through, it's the barback.

Because that's their job.

To have everyone in that bar's back.

There's a special place in all our hearts for the unsung hero. Rarely do we get to experience what it's like to shed our ego long enough, and unassuming enough, to play that role.

Barbacks do it every shift.

They are the heart and soul of our bars.

Not only that, but becoming a great barback is also the best
first step you can take in building a successful bartending career.

The best first step. Period.

And you have everything, right now, within your own power
to be great. All you have to do is bust your ass and be completely of service to those around you.

My interview with Pedro Shanahan perfectly illustrates the
mindset of how to be a great barback. It also shows the power
of humility and nobility—and how those two values can trickle
down the line and eventually not only shape a bar but represent it.

There is no ceiling for the amount of respect a barback can
earn from their bar team. You do it right, and it won't be long
until you'll be sought after to move up to bartending.

Now, it's true that the leap from barback to bartender is a big
one. It's a big raise with many more benefits—and sometimes
temptations. But for most of us, it's the dream-shot opportunity we got into the business for in the first place.

Now, it's your direct responsibility to build and maintain regulars. To take care of your community around you. To flex the
skillset you've been sharpening throughout your journey so far.

To finally delve into the full power of Pouring with Heart.

If you've received or are on track for the bartender call up, congratulations. You've been knighted. You've paid your dues and made the bar a better place for it.

Now it's time to take your rightful seat at the table.

CHAPTER SEVEN

HOW TO BECOME A
~~GREAT BARTENDER~~
LEGEND

"I've learned that people will forget what you said,
people will forget what you did, but
people will never forget how you made them feel."

—Maya Angelou

If you bought this book, there's a good chance this chapter is the reason why. Maybe you want to be a bartender. Maybe you want to be a better one.

And why not? They're the ones with the magic.

I am not, nor have I ever been, a bartender. Not professionally, anyway.

But damn if I haven't been around them my entire life. And damn if they aren't *fire*.

Like a conductor walking onstage, the spotlight finds them the second they step foot behind the bar. Anticipation heightens from those in the crowd holding their breath as they raise two tins in the air, pausing *ever so slightly* to gauge the energy of the audience before their performance begins.

They can feel everything around them.

Always mindful. Always present. Their ready, capable hands commence—rattling ice in a soothing rhythm that gets the crowd out of their heads and into their bodies.

Being in the presence of a great bartender is intoxicating.

They have power. They have poise. They have charisma and charm. They are the keepers of the booze. And the unique attention that comes with that responsibility.

They are flirted with, cursed at, negotiated, pitched, propositioned, praised, lamented, and envied.

They're rock stars.

Which is a hell of a life. And if that's *your* life, great.

Pay attention. This chapter will make you *even better*.

I'll show you exactly what you're capable of when you add Pouring with Heart to your rock star résumé. How you can become the kind of bartender that even the rock stars in our industry look up to.

How you can become...*a legend.*

BECOMING A LEGEND

The good news is, it all goes back to Pouring with Heart. The bad news is, there's no script for it. Even if there were a canned playbook for the magic behind the bartenders we love, it would only cheapen it. Because real magic can't be confined to a cheat sheet you reference while stumbling through the daily specials. Neither can empathy. Or things like pride, passion, or sincerity.

Values don't mean anything if they're just vomited from a soulless thesaurus of forced trigger words.

The legends in this business know that.

They inspire others by being *themselves*, making it personal by tapping into their hearts in their own way. And in doing so, others discover the energy they release—a warmth, a goodwill—that is so rare and so unique to themselves that it creates a connection nothing short of magic.

Your magic will be the same.

Only you know how to be yourself. Only you know how to access your heart and express it the way you do with your closest friends and family.

How we treat the people we care about most is more than special. *It's our magic.*

Legends bring that magic and warmth with them to work every day.

Without restriction.

Because they know this gift they *choose* to share has the power to make someone else's life better.

When you *do right* by your guests and your community. When you take care of them. When you find any and every little thing you can do to enrich their lives—if only for that brief moment in time—you are Pouring with Heart.

You're also starting to pour like a legend.

But it doesn't happen without the first step.

INTENTION

Pouring with Heart begins, each shift, with having *conscious intention.*

Are you ready for your shift? Are you carrying any emotional or psychological baggage that's going to inhibit your ability to be fully of service to your guests and bar team?

Your bag of bullshit is just as important as the next person's.

But that's not what your guests came in for. Quite the opposite, actually. When your personal shit gets in the way of your job, you've failed for that shift.

A lot of bartenders fall into this trap. Sometimes we can't right the ship of our personal life before getting behind the bar that night. It's hard to focus on being of service when our mind is back in a blowout fight with our landlord.

Some bartenders turn to booze and drugs to try to circumvent having the wrong intention. Thinking a shot here and there or doing a line mid-shift is going to help them "lock in" and "keep the party going." That's just putting a Band-Aid on things, trying to mask how they feel inside.

At best.

The thing about compensating for feelings with drugs and alcohol is, well, it usually ends poorly.

I'm not saying you have to be a saint to be a legend.

But legends pride themselves on their positive intention. They're constantly, actively thinking about it. Prioritizing the feelings of their guests before their own.

Any of us can do this.

I promise it's not rarified air, reserved for the 1 percent who have had the hand of God touch their tins. It's for the driven, yes, but mostly, it's for those who embody Pouring with Heart. I've seen my fair share of legends go from misfits to instant hall of famers.

And furthermore, it can be done on DAY ONE.

Because it's a choice. It's a mindset. If you go about things the right way, set your desired intention, and tap into your heart every day, you'll lay the groundwork necessary to cement your status as a legend.

Now, whether that's becoming a legend within your own staff, a local legend in your community, or a world-renowned legend that never pays for a drink again, that's up to the bar gods.

There's a legend born in almost every bar.

If it's not you yet, then look around. It's the bartender on staff that's *figured it out*. Their service line is probably the longest. Other bartenders eye them throughout the night to mimic their style. And they've got a genuine smile on their face when they're dealing.

They look like they're constantly *in the zone*.

They don't just tap in and out of their gift when they see someone's watching. Go out of their way when they're *in the mood* or because their friends are in the bar.

A legend is always locked in on their guest's experience. Even if the guest sucks.

Because a shitty guest is not an excuse to be an asshole. Most legends aren't *also* known for being pricks. They're also not the bartender at the end of the night hammered and duking it out with a customer who got under their skin.

Legends lift people up. One of your great honors as a bartender is getting to be the ultimate team player. In fact, you can usually spot the legend by looking for the person in the bar who makes everyone around them better. Makes everybody look good, from their bar team to the guests who make their way in the bar.

One guest at a time, every time.

There's no greater achievement than to Pour with so much goddamn Heart that even the biggest jerkoff customer in the room is now loosening up, having a good time, and no longer disrespecting those around them.

People rally around a legend. They feed off their energy, personality, and vibe. They're enthralled by how they handle adversity. How they thrive in the spotlight. How they can make a person's night. How they can make a thousand people's night, *each night*.

*"The most important goal of a bartender's job
is to make sure that every guest leaves the bar happier
than when they walked in."*

—Gary Regan, legend and author, *The Joy of Mixology*

More on Gary later.

COCKTAILS CONFESSED

Once again, in the words of legend and author Eric Alperin, "Attending to a guest in the environment is more important than cocktails. People remember how they felt over what they had."

Epic, earth-shattering, light-your-hair-on-fire cocktails are awesome. But a legend will tell you straight up.

Making great drinks isn't good enough.

As important as ingredients, balance, and recipes are to our craft, they're still just bartending basics. They're extensions of a skillset that can be easily taught and vesseled over time. They rely mostly on hand–eye coordination, muscle memory, and practice to make perfect. Dare I say: it's robotic.

Anyone with a jigger, a little practice, and an okay drink recipe can figure out how to make a cocktail.

A "good" bartender delivers drinks consistently. They have the classics down—or at least the staple cocktails listed on their bar's menu—and produce quality, balanced cocktails with confidence and speed.

A "great" bartender takes these kernels and executes them *when it counts*. They are reliable in the moment and perform with precision, no matter how high-stress, high-stake, or high-pressure filled the stage.

But we didn't read this far to become okay, good, or great.

We're here to become a legend.

And a legend knows that a great drink, though an essential part of the bartending package, is just the beginning. Because getting a great drink isn't a guest's aspiration.

It's their *expectation*.

What they *don't* expect is that their drink is Poured with Heart.

Remember, before a guest orders their first round, they've likely done their homework on your bar. They've probably Googled, Yelped, maybe even gone down a rabbit hole of blogs about your spot. There's a chance they made plans with their friends that took almost a week to coordinate. Maybe they even worked up the guts to ask a special someone out that night. They likely picked out an outfit, braved the weather, and paid for a fucking Uber to get there.

All that shit goes into their first drink order.

Recognizing it, like the legends do, makes that guest *feel* like their effort was worth it.

That's why these guests come back.

With more friends, more special someones, more Ubers.

And when they do, most of them won't remember the cocktail you poured them. But they'll remember how you made them feel when you did.

Sasha Petraske knew that.

Those who had the pleasure of being mentored by the legend would tell you what Sasha loved most was how bars, and everyone working in them, had the opportunity to make people *feel special*.

More on Sasha later.

POURING WITH HEART FATIGUE

Tapping into your heart with every person you meet at your bar is taxing. Bartenders have feelings, emotions, and patience that wanes, just like anybody else.

Fatigue is a real thing.

When a bartender's making cocktails, they're accessing their mind to repeat learned motor functions at a rapid pace. Like painting a fence or throwing a fastball, the task is mostly mechanical.

But when a bartender is making cocktails *and* Pouring with Heart, they're accessing something more. They're combining the mechanical with the intangible—operating from the engine in their chest along with the computer in their head. The engine that is your heart takes a hell of a lot more energy to run than the mind.

So, yes. Even legends experience fatigue.

The difference is that they don't lose their shit when they're *spent* and some asshole touches on their last nerve. Instead, they reset.

Sometimes resetting means taking a step back. Taking some time off. There's no shame in getting a shift covered for a much-needed "breather."

But usually, it just means doubling down on your service. Grounding yourself to be present with your guest.

Pouring with Heart, baby.

Because often in life, the way out…is also the *way in.*

When a legend feels down, you won't find them sidestepping their guests. For them, the obstacle is the way. They don't disappear in the middle of a shift to cope. Run to the back every eight minutes for a smoke break. Burn a joint on the rooftop or rip a line in the stairwell.

Legends do the opposite.

They lean into their guests. Because their guests give them fuel.

Remember, serotonin spreads like wildfire. The more a legend gives to their guests, the more they get in return. And it beats any elixir out there for getting our minds back on track. It's one of the coolest parts of the magic.

When the other side is in on the trick.

ATTRIBUTES OF A LEGEND

Legendary bartenders stay completely present with the people right in front of them. They put their heart and soul into being of service. They Pour with Heart with impeccable consistency.

When we peel back the curtain a bit, we find that these legends share a set of attributes that you can aspire to while you're on the clock.

Every legend exercises these attributes in their own unique way. It's kind of the best part.

I'll share some staples I've picked up on over the last twenty-five years as I've had the pleasure of sitting front and center to some of the greatest to ever do it.

THEY'RE GRACIOUS

The difference between being nice and being gracious is that *nice* can be faked. Being gracious is something genuine. It takes more time. More effort. More honesty.

More humility.

Being gracious means operating from a place of kindness first.

Now obviously, shit happens, and things aren't always ideal. But to be truly of service to others, we cannot let those difficulties compromise our graciousness.

We aren't meant to reserve our good grace for when we're in a good mood.

We're meant to be kind *always*.

The reason being, people don't often let their guard down... *until you do.*

When a legend opens up with their guest from the heart, a guest recognizes it quickly. This is usually where some solid bonding begins. Where a great customer experience becomes possible.

Creating a sense of welcome makes a stranger feel like you're opening up your home for their safe passage. Being gracious lets them know they belong in your home.

That they are a *part* of your home.

Legends don't look at new people across the bar as strangers; they see amazing people they haven't met yet. Strangers give us our greatest opportunities as bartenders. Any one of these people could become one of your best regulars. Maybe even a close friend. The mission to turn strangers into regulars requires our full attention and belief in them as good people.

NOTE: It's impossible to be gracious and read off a script. To be truly generous in conversation. Genuine in inquiry. Legends don't regurgitate campy lines from the recesses of their "training."

That doesn't cut it.

As people, we can't be taught to be kind.

That was up to our parents. And/or the work we've done in our life to let go of anger and resentment. At the root of which is having empathy for others.

It's a loop. Kindness begins with empathy. Empathy, in turn, generates feelings of kindness.

Remember, our customers all have problems too. They might be recovering from a horrible day at work or going through the recent loss of a loved one. Anticipating that about guests, knowing that they're coming into the bar for more than just a drink, sets the legends apart from the rest.

"Empathy is a real-life human superpower," according to sociologist Dr. Ali Hill. "When we truly empathize with others, we come as close to reading minds as humans can get. When we empathize, we can actually feel what the other person is feeling, and when we can feel what someone else feels, then we can inherently understand what they're trying to communicate."

Legends listen to their customers and visualize themselves in their shoes in order to better understand their feelings and deliver beyond their expectations.

Furthermore, they read the subtext.

A guest will tell you all kinds of things about themselves through their body language alone: their mood, their day, their demeanor. It's easier than you think if you're looking for it.

Does the customer appear hurried? Stressed? Are they wet from the rain or freezing from the cold outside? Are they curiously looking around the bar? Are they bored?

Addressing a guest's needs before they ask for them sets a tone of comfort and safety. Ensuring them that they are at the right bar. And that they are with the right bartender.

Lastly, legends aren't afraid to show a little gratitude for their guests' effort.

A customer could drink anywhere in the world. Anywhere else in the city. Hell, at their own bar at home. But instead, they waited in line to saddle up and be served by that legend.

These people made plans, got dressed up, and rallied their closest to be there with that legend.

What a sign of respect. What a show of love.

Which is why the last thing a legend will do is take their customers for granted.

For a legend, the guest is everything. Without guests, they have nothing. No job. No purpose. No music in an empty concert hall.

Legends are rock stars, yes. But they don't play for the love of the music.

They play for the crowd.

They reach into their souls and strum their instruments to the heavens to give their guests the best damn night of their life. They kick some ass, and then they line up again and bring 'em back for an encore. Making it clear to the guest that the time spent with them was well invested.

That's how legends roll.

When you stare past your well at a sea of customers, consider how each guest had to overcome their own personal set of obstacles to be there that night. The ones you see staring back at you are the ones that overcame them all. And when they did, they *chose you* to drink with.

As Jay-Z used to say to the audience before every "Izzo" performance:

"Welcome ladies and gentlemen to the 8th wonder of the world. The flow of the century, oh it's timeless. HOV'! Thanks for coming out tonight. You coulda been anywhere in the world, but you're here with me. I appreciate that."

—Jay-Z, "Izzo (H.O.V.A)," *The Blueprint*

THEY EMBRACE THE MOMENT

The highest form of respect we can show another person is to give them our undivided attention. To let them know that we are completely present.

That we are with them.

To do that, legends listen. Carefully.

Most of us spend the time another person is speaking thinking about the next thing *we* want to say. If you're doing that, you're liable to miss something. I take that back. You're guaranteed to miss something.

A legendary bartender doesn't miss a goddamn thing. They want to catch every word before they speak so they're crystal clear about what their customer wants. Because it's impossible to meet expectations, let alone surpass them, if they don't truly understand what their guest needs.

Sometimes a guest will come into a bar without the faintest clue of what it is they want or need.

A legend knows how to get them there.

No one does this better than the legends of Japan.

I've never felt more appreciated in a city than I did when I had the pleasure of visiting Tokyo. It was like being able to visit a half dozen of the best bars in the world...all in one night. For those who don't think pride and nobility exist in hospitality. In service. In bars...

Japan will make you a believer.

It's remarkable how their legends can be so completely of service to their guests. Their desire to serve not only elevates your spirit but theirs as well. Every cocktail tastes a little more incredible than the last thanks to their ultimate attention to detail, precision, and presentation. But mostly because of the care they take when you're in their presence. They don't need to ask you if you liked your cocktail.

They study the nuances in your face.

Keep in mind that all this is with zero expectation of being tipped (receiving tips is taboo in Japan).

Japanese legends give all the credit to Ichigo Ichie: "One opportunity, one encounter."

This proverb describes a mindset of appreciation for the unrepeatable nature of the moment. Another way to think of it is "one time, one meeting." For me, it's the ultimate "moment of truth" between bartender and guest. It's the best opportunity we have for building regulars in our bars.

Ichigo Ichie is rooted in Buddhist teachings and has long been practiced by the Japanese during ancient tea ceremonies as a way for hosts to keep their focus on service and the care of their guests top of mind.

It reminds us to cherish the interaction. For no interaction will ever happen in the same way again.

Even when the same people return to the same place—because a particular moment can never be repeated—each time we serve someone, *it is a once-in-a-lifetime experience.*

Imagine adopting this mentality every shift. If you treated each cocktail, each moment with each guest, like it was your last.

This way of thinking allows Japanese legends to tap into their hearts and honor their guests with extraordinary service. Again, not for the *tip*. But for that specific moment in time.

This is Pouring with Heart in such a beautiful way.

Regardless of how great or small that moment in time might be for you, you *never know* how important that time is to your guest.

John DiJulius III said it best in his book *The Relationship Economy*: "Never lose sight of the impact you make on other people in any given moment. The choice you make to smile (or not), to follow through (or not), to be empathetic (or not), makes a bigger difference than you will ever know."

These moments are precious. And more importantly, they're finite.

Life's too short to burn 'em.

THEY KILL THE EGO

Legends begin reading their guests the second they walk into the bar. They have their eyes, their ears, their taste buds primed to help navigate a customer where they want to go.

They're always asking questions. Reading body language. Listening and gathering information. And then making informed recommendations on behalf of their guests based on the information they've paid such close attention to.

They indebt themselves to their guests to gain every advantage they can to better serve them. They do this over and over again, and not just during their interactions. On the subway ride home. Relaxing at home over a cocktail themselves. The guest and how to better meet their needs is a constant conversation they have with themselves.

Because they know when they're bartending that it's their job to figure out what their guests' needs are.

Not what "their" needs are.

Legendary bartenders fuel other egos. Not their own.

Moments of self-praise and self-importance may do wonders for you outside the bar. I get it; feeding the ego feels good. But when you're behind the bar, the ego does nothing for your guest.

What it *does do* is hamper your ability to Pour with Heart.

It puts a roadblock up between your guest and the incredible night they want to have at your bar. The ego *makes the choice* for a guest versus guiding them toward the right decision on their own. The ego wants verbal/monetary credit for a delicious cocktail versus being content with seeing a guest's face light up after their first sip.

The ego wants it to be clear that *they* are special and the guest is lucky to be in their special presence. Versus...*the guest* is special and it's an honor to be of service.

Scenario A

Guest: *"Hi, can I get six shots of psycho cinnamon blazing hot whiskey for me and my friends?"*

Ego-driven bartender: *"Sure, if you're an asshole! We don't sell that crap here. What kind of bar do you think this is? What kind of bartender do you think I am? (Turns to bartender next to him) Do you believe this fucking guy? (Back to guest, now laughing) I'll pour you six shots of a ten-year-old single barrel, and that's the best I can do. But honestly, this probably isn't the bar for you, buddy."*

Classic example of the bartender making the situation all about themselves. They have their opinion on the drink order in question. They think it's beneath them or beneath their bar. And rather than look at the situation from the guest's perspective, all the bartender can hear is their own ego being attacked, insulted, or trapped by its insecurities.

Scenario B

Guest: *"Hi, can I get six shots of psycho cinnamon blazing hot whiskey for me and my friends?"*

Legend: *"First of all, thank you for bringing six friends into the bar tonight. That's awesome–what are we celebrating? About that whiskey, we don't carry that particular bottle in house because we don't get too many orders for it, but what I can do is make sure you get something delicious and fast for all your friends. If you've got your heart set on cinnamon, we can find something with a similar profile. I have this amazing ten-year single barrel a lot of us behind the bar absolutely love right now. It's not psycho cinnamon, but it is overproof, starts sweet with a spicy finish, and is pretty close in price point."*

If you feed the ego for instant gratification by hitting the guest over the head and humiliating them, you can be assured there's definitely an asshole in the bar.

And it's you.

Lastly, legends train and continue to learn endlessly, but they don't showboat their knowledge. If you are truly the best, you don't need to tell anyone you are. Your actions speak to it.

"The moment any pleasure is taken at demonstrating one's skill at swordsmanship, all possibility of true swordsmanship is lost."

—Miyamoto Musashi, philosopher, strategist, writer, and rōnin

The guest doesn't need a painfully boring tour of Scotland before they get a chance to order a couple of vodka sodas. Unless, of course, they want to hear about the rickhouses and what the smell is like on the Isle of Orkney. Then by all means, wow us all.

Humility is so important. Even the greatest bartenders of all time will concede "it's only a drink." The best in the game don't take themselves, or their drinks, too seriously. Instead, they take pride in their job. Pride in their bar. And pride in their bar family.

All great things we love about our legends.

Because when the booze is flowing, the music is blaring, and the stress is climbing, the last thing we need is our ego ringing the ego bell.

What we need is to get off our fucking high horse and put our heart and soul into serving.

THEY ARE THE BRIDGE

Legends are anchors in the night. They are the compass, the guide, the map for the strayed.

And when a traveler finds them and tiptoes into their world, they make it their responsibility to provide a steady bridge for them.

They use their exquisite attention to detail. Their communication skills. Turn the canvas that is their bar top into a runway for slinging cocktails that blow fucking minds.

But that's the easy part of the bridge.

The important part...is the connection.

When you're being served by a legend—*you know*–above all else, that they are looking out for you.

Their goal is to provide you with a good time. A safe time. To be a conduit to your happiness. Legends know within seconds whether you're thirsty, lonely, horny, cold, bored, celebrating, nervous, or in pain. And they have an empathy Rolodex to accommodate any situation.

People who frequent bars are human beings before they're customers. Which means, like all of us, they come with a wide array of feelings and thoughts and emotions. In order to match their empathy with the various energies of so many guests, legends build a new, distinctive bridge with each of them.

Customers can tell the difference between a bartender who is talking *at* them. And a bartender who is talking *to* them. The former approach annoys a guest. The latter enamors them.

At this point, the guest is all theirs.

A legend exudes in seconds that they have your back. That they can be trusted and relied upon and will be a rock for you all night. What better feeling is there when we go out than to have that kind of support?

Bartenders that Pour with Heart have the opportunity to make someone's day, *every day*.

Shit, a lot of jobs pay us to *ruin* people's fucking day. Imagine writing parking tickets for a paycheck. Serving divorce papers. Or denying loans. Dashing hopes and dreams. Reaching into their chest and gutting them for a living.

It feels so good being on the right side of that one.

I love it when I'm in a new town. A new bar. And the bartender goes full concierge on me. They tell me where they like to drink in their free time. Let me in on a secret back alley spot they know about. Where to find the best slice in town.

Or a taco truck after three a.m.

A legend loves to link people together. They know that being the bridge for their community bonds their bar with its city and culture.

Whether that means giving up some of that city's best-kept secrets. Or *keeping them*.

There's no end to the support you can lend as the bridge. A little practice and soon it'll feel like second nature. You won't remember what it's like to *not* go the distance for your guest. With every guest. Because you'll get to witness the overwhelming impact it has on them.

It's life changing.

Suddenly realizing you have it in you to make people feel damn good.

There's a special side of you that gets unlocked when you achieve this level of service. A confidence that shines from the ability to communicate and connect with others. To leave a lasting impression on someone that they *feel*.

And though it may begin at your bar, that confidence usually spills over into your personal life and comes in handy with friends, family, and sometimes the strangers you fall head over heels for.

LEGENDS WHO POUR WITH HEART
So far, we've discussed some common attributes inherent among the bartenders we love.

The legends.

Now, it's time we meet them. Let's go to the Hall of Fame. The Mount Rushmore of Pouring with Heart.

Each bartender on this list comes with their own magic. And when they Poured with Heart, they did it *their own way*. Let's take a peek at how they did it. And what made their magic so special.

What made them legends.

MIGUEL ALONSO
"Miguel Alonso is a legend."

That's what you'll hear while waiting in an absurdly long line of regulars all trying to get up to his bar. Miguel is an example of a bartender who became a legend within our bar family by building thousands—and thousands—of regulars by Pouring with Heart. They don't just visit him routinely.

They visit him religiously.

Miguel started as a barback with zero experience behind the bar.

He was *forty-eight*.

Seven years later, he's our most popular bartender. Every night, the biggest line in the bar leads to his station. People wait patiently to be served by him despite adjacent bartenders having few to no one in their lines at all. And it's not because his drinks are necessarily any better than those other bartenders'.

It's because Miguel knows how to make every customer feel like a million bucks.

He has a gift for connecting with everyone who walks into the bar. He has thousands of Instagram followers who regularly check in, wanting to know the time of his next shift so they can get back in line to be served by him again.

Miguel has absolutely mastered Pouring with Heart. I'd share more words about him myself, but his are much better. Here's part of an interview I did with the legend from Heroica Ciudad de Cuautla, Morelos, Mexico:

For me, it's something fun because I really love what I do. I really enjoy it and I try to be of service to everybody. I'm happy and I'm glad I have a lot of regulars. I don't see the customer as a customer. I see the new customer as a friend. And when they are a regular, I see them like family.

When it's not too busy, Miguel gives hugs to his regulars as they make it to his bar top.

He is always sure to thank the customers personally for coming in to see him. While most bartenders are in the alley smoking a cigarette and catching up on text messages during their breaks, Miguel leaps out from behind the bar during his to mingle and make sure his guests feel the love.

Miguel looks and does nothing like the "successful" proto-type bartender Hollywood portrays in TV and movies. He doesn't check a single stereotypical box, and yet his ability to establish connection with his guests trumps nearly every other bartender that does. He *CRUSHES* tips. And because most bartenders pool their tips, his popularity puts good bread in his entire team's pocket, as well.

It's a great feeling to be able to give back to your bar team that way.

Miguel's ability to make people feel special breaks down all walls. All stereotypes. It fosters diversity, inclusion, and unity in his bar. And it proves that anything is possible in yours.

But as much as Miguel's countless regulars appear to come back into the bar for him, the truth is that they're really coming back in for themselves.

Because of how great Miguel makes them feel. *AND THAT'S OKAY.*

In fact, that's what we want. What we ALL want. Miguel's people come back because they want to feel good again. The way they felt the last time they were in his bar. Knowing they have a place where they know someone is going to trigger that serotonin in them.

Get the positivity and the good times flowing.

Miguel makes *even me* feel like his best friend. The first time I met him, I too stood in a ridiculously long line. When we were introduced, he sprung out from behind the bar and showered me with his energy and enthusiasm. Even the friend I was with that night was taken aback by the royal treatment he gave us. But the best part is, after we got our drink and moved about the bar, looking back toward Miguel's well, it was plain to see that he was doing that with *everybody*.

WITHOUT watering anything down. He was genuine and authentic with every interaction. He knew his guests' names, their family stories, the little things that were going on in their lives. And then, for all the love he put out there, he was getting it back tenfold.

People truly can't get enough of him. As he said:

I try to pour the right way, with corazòn. It's probably the secret. I try to make them feel safe and comfortable in the bar to really enjoy whatever they want to drink. When you serve from the heart, the customers love it.

Miguel sets his intention the same every shift.

He is going to treat you as a friend the minute you walk into the bar. If he sees you come back into the bar, then you are family.

That personal care and attention has built Miguel a mountain of regulars and fans who adore him. I am so proud of the career he has built with us. He brings joy to his community and makes our world a better place for it.

IVY MIX

I would estimate 90 percent of how a person feels about your cocktail is determined by how they feel about *YOU* before they sip it. If this is true, then it's a big reason why no one's ever said a bad thing about an Ivy Mix cocktail. Ivy's greatest strength is her contagious love for the drinks she serves. When she is behind the bar, everyone in the place knows it. She's that electric. The energy that reverberates across the bar top and out into the crowd that gathers as close to her station as possible.

Ivy is a magnet.

Her heart beats to the drum of every customer, making sure each guest she interacts with is having a good time and enjoying themselves in her bar. She *lives* off the reactions she gets from her award-winning drinks and being of world-class service to those she serves them to.

But above all else, Ivy believes cocktailing should be fun. And that a bartender's relationship with their guests ought to reflect that:

It makes me feel good to give people something that maybe they didn't even know they wanted. It makes me feel good when people want to spend their evening sitting in front of my bar. It literally re-fuels my fire, and it was that way before I was even making cocktails! Even when I was just, like, pouring shots and beers. I love it when people want to come in.

I couldn't agree with her more.

There are a thousand ways you can fail when being of service to a guest. But if your objective begins and ends with making the experience enjoyable for them, you can almost never lose. When your heart is in the right place, like Ivy's, it helps you come across as trustworthy and likable.

For Ivy, charismatic.

When Ivy stares back at you with a wall of spirits behind her, she is listening first and creating second. From start to finish, she makes the experience about her guest, and not the other way around.

Ivy's accomplishments tower above most of her contemporaries'. But where she really sets herself apart from other legends is in her humility.

And her humanity.

I worry about things all the time. But it's proof to me that I'm not a horrible sack of shit when people come in and they want to be around me and my bar. You know, it just brings out the love. I think we all have a little bit of that in us. It's great to make people's day. All right, it's the best. I think the ability to connect by serving others is at the root of our business. And that people that believe in that, you know, they find themselves through serving other people. Everyone loves to talk about the cocktails. But for me it's the challenge and creativity involved in being able to engineer something perfect for someone–that is just for that person, in that time and place, and that moment alone.

Ivy's ability to empathize with her guests is off the charts. She's the blueprint for the kind of bartender who doesn't take herself too seriously, despite being one of the best in the country.

When I say "the best," I mean Ivy Mix literally won the award for Best Bartender in America at Tales of the Cocktail, 2018–2019. Yet still, there's not an ounce of pretentiousness about the way she shares her gift with the world. The same could be said about the way she taps into her heart and shares that with us too.

One of my favorite things about Ivy is how she persevered against an uphill battle of criticism to get to the top of her career. Sadly, people don't always recognize greatness. Sometimes greatness is so overwhelming and unlike anything they've ever seen before that its comprehension is almost impossible for them to grasp.

Or sometimes, they're just dicks.

And refuse to give proper recognition to the best person doing the best fucking job.

Ivy knew in her heart there was a beauty to her hospitality approach. And if those in the industry couldn't see that, or couldn't understand her style of service, then she would just have to show it to them.

All of them.

She didn't second-guess herself and cave under their scrutiny.

She Poured with Heart.

It was only a matter of time before Ivy's infectious hospitality and knack for lighting up a room would catch fire. And when it did, she became one of the biggest names in the industry.

Speed Rack, an international bartending competition Ivy co-founded, has made a tremendous name for itself by showcasing some of the top female bartenders on the planet. This venture has raised millions of dollars for breast cancer research and elevated the landscape of women behind the bar throughout the world.

Ivy is a self-driven agent of change with unparalleled tenacity. She's embraced and loved by those around her in every city she goes. Especially if that city, or town, winds up being in a Latin American country.

If you ever find yourself sipping on some Latin spirits at an island bar off the coast of Belize and you stumble upon the best drink of your life, you might be enjoying an Ivy Mix original.

I hope the "fuel" Ivy refers to getting from her customers is something that never runs out.

GARY REGAN
Eighteen-time author and bartending legend Gary Regan did it his way.

A man who first tended bar in his parents' pub at fourteen years old, left England for America, and brought the pulse for a cocktail revolution and a twisted sense of British humor when he did.

Regan used that humor and extremely thick British accent to connect with and charm his customers. If he ever felt he was losing touch with the crowd, he'd put on an excessive amount of eyeshadow to better attract attention to his eyes. His way of drawing a richer, deeper sense of eye contact between him and his guests.

Our very own Salvador Dalí of the New York bar scene.

Gary's extensive literary catalogue includes the iconic *Joy of Mixology*. An indelible, thoughtfully written cocktail book Regan uses to offer an honest portrayal of the ebbs and flows of the craft of bartending, including the sacred dance between bartender and guest.

However, despite possessing an unbound knowledge of cocktails in his head—and having turned that knowledge into a book most people in the industry still refer to as their bible today—Gary Regan was as unpretentious about making drinks as they come.

In fact, shortly before he passed, Gary told the *New York Times*: "Drinks are not the main reason to tend bar. The most important thing a bartender can do is make people smile."

Gary Regan made plenty of souls smile under his watch. He stood out in the industry as being someone completely peculiar, but at the same time, completely authentic. Completely genuine.

Completely himself.

He was so comfortable in his skin when interacting with his guests. Almost egoless at times, happy to serve you anything your heart unequivocally desired. Whether that was the perfect Manhattan or a shot of Jack, it didn't matter in the least from one of the great forefathers of modern cocktailing.

What was most important to Gary was setting the intention for his service before each shift. Something he would notoriously take five minutes to do before getting behind the bar each night.

If you approach every situation that goes down in your bar with the intention of seeing past what might appear to be nasty, and understanding instead how love can prevail, then you'll always end up guiding the situation to the happiest ending possible.

I love this tip from Gary. Making it a priority to take a few minutes to sit quietly and set the positive intentions he needed in order to be completely of service to his guests that night.

As much personality as Gary Regan had, he wasn't one to showboat. He wasn't a grandstander or a Mr. Main Event. For him, Pouring with Heart came about through mindfulness. He could propel himself onto a spiritual plane in order to rid himself of the baggage clinging to him throughout his day.

Truly freeing himself to be wholly available for his customers and their needs.

He understood the power of connection with others. He knew the impact he made when he made a stranger's day. And, as echoed by Ivy Mix's sentiments, it was in these moments of devotion to being of service to others that he was able to find a little bit of himself.

And the peace that came along with that.

DALE DEGROFF

The most important thing–the thing that needs to happen immediately–is eye contact. When a guest walks through the door, you give them a wave and a smile, even if the bar is three or four deep. It's the difference between keeping and losing a customer.

Words of wisdom from arguably the most famous living bartender in the world.

Dale DeGroff is an unrelenting raconteur. He has the ability to walk into a new environment and, within seconds, hold court wherever he goes.

And he's damn good at it.

Whether it's his gift of gab, his stature, or his presence…Dale's ability to fearlessly step into a cold room—*and will it warm*—makes him one of the most adored legends we have.

Dale's most endearing quality behind the bar, like the rest of the legends on this list, has nothing to do with cocktails. It's the picture he paints with his words. His body language. The deep connection that radiates effortlessly between him and the person right in front of him.

And most of all, his remarkable way of making you, the guest, feel like you're the only person in the bar. It's his love language. His unique way of showing his appreciation to people. As great as he is at telling stories, what Dale loves most is to *LISTEN* to other people's tales.

He loves life. He loves people. And he loves sharing laughs.

In our world, Dale is royalty. "King Cocktail," they call him. Fit for a man who started the Museum of the American Cocktail. And though his presence is intimidating, when I walked up to him for the first time, he immediately put me at ease. The same way he's done with hundreds of thousands of guests before me.

He looked me straight in the eye. He gave me the impression I was the only person in the room that mattered to him. He invited my presence in, along with the words I would speak. He made me feel, instantly, that what I had to say was important. Even though I can't remember to this day what it was.

That's the thing about a legend. It doesn't matter what I said. It matters how Dale made me feel.

Dale's insistence on quality and innovation didn't just lead to a cocktail renaissance in this country. It also led to a renaissance of legendary bartenders following in his footsteps. Suddenly, the bar world, and its humble tavern keepers, barbacks, and bartenders, could no longer be sneezed at.

Bars and bartenders started to be seen and respected the way they *used to be*.

Dale showed us all another way—a better way—to make cocktails. He ushered us out of the dark ages, freed us of the McDonald's effect, and raised the bar from canned syrups to quality beverages we could geek out about together.

The novel concept of *fresh*.

From crap to craft, Dale helped reset the American palate.

Suddenly, we were free to try new things. To bend recipes with a brand-new armament of ingredients. Tweak renditions of classic cocktails. All in the spirit of improving the guest experience.

Dale provided a clean canvas for us to play with.

He loves cocktails. His country. And his customers. All three are evidenced in an iconic passage from his book, *The Craft of the Cocktail:*

> *The cocktail is, in a word, American. It's as American as jazz, apple pie, and baseball; and as diverse, colorful, and big as America itself. Indeed, it could even be argued that the cocktail is a metaphor for the American people: It is a composite beverage, and we are a composite people.*

When our bar family first faced adversity, breaking ground in Downtown LA, Dale was one of the few that stood up for us. He made us feel confident we were doing something *right*.

I'll never forget that.

SASHA PETRASKE

An hour into a bartender's training session with Sasha, I noticed we hadn't even picked up a bottle. I was lucky enough to sit in on his training, and when I did, I couldn't help but notice each hour going by without him saying the word "cocktail."

Let alone actually making one.

Sasha just had a *different* approach.

Everything was about the guest. His training reflected his philosophy.

Read the guest. Empathize. Understand.

Do whatever it takes to ensure you've given them the best experience of their life.

He believed people inherently deserved the right to be treated with integrity and respect. And though he was a savant at creating and reinterpreting cocktails—perfecting their balance and temperature with meticulous abandon—for Sasha, it was genuinely *never* about the drink.

We make cocktails as well as can be made, and that should not be such a big deal... If a guest would like to discuss ingredients or a drink's origins, by all means they should be indulged. But the pursuit is not to thrill with knowledge; it is to serve with consideration.

Petraske was motivated by the reaction of his guest, hellbent on them leaving the bar happier than when they arrived.

His power...was in his humility.

In 2004, I found myself bellied up to one of the most fabled drinking establishments in the world.

Milk & Honey, New York City.

I'm inside a cathedral of cocktails. Drinks all around that didn't transcend just the globe but the history of our time on it as well.

Until some schlep beside me, graced by Sasha's full attention and presence, orders a Diet Coke.

I was floored.

The audacity of asking Babe Ruth to bunt.

But Sasha didn't see it that way. He wouldn't see it that way in a thousand years.

Now, it was clear there was no Diet Coke in the most famous bar in the world. But that didn't dictate how Sasha was going to Pour with Heart.

He said, "Thanks for your order. I'll get to it in just a couple of moments."

And promptly slipped out of the bar, ran to the liquor store, bought a can of Diet Coke, came back, and poured the soda over a fancy, hand-chipped shard of ice and served it.

Sasha's one-on-one with customers transformed a lost moment in time into an event you'd never forget.

The guy would take three days sometimes to plan and make a fucking ice cube for one goddamn cocktail. For one drink to be served.

For one guest.

They were that important to him.

He inspired people to be better, to treat people better, and to aim to do so through graciousness for others. He fueled the spirits of a lot of bartenders who still shout his praise, not through his name, but by his philosophy. His wisdom and teachings. His presence.

His way of the craft.

When you're always onstage, the customer is always watching. But Sasha gave us insight on how to watch *back*.

He studied every little detail of human interactions. He practiced and conversed about nuances in people's behavior over and over to make sure he had the human part of the human connection right.

That needed to be perfected long before the cocktail was.

To Sasha, Pouring with Heart was the standard.

His intention was always clear: "How can I transport you right now with my tins, my tools. How can I better listen to you, better understand your story?"

He would ask how you felt in the moment, and then make you the perfect cocktail to reflect your mood. Most times, there was no menu with Sasha. You ordered by sharing with him how your day was, and then he'd find a way to translate the rest through spirit.

In order to lift yours.

CHAPTER EIGHT

MOVING INTO LEADERSHIP POSITIONS

"Never look down on anybody unless you're helping them up."
—Jesse Jackson

So far, you've learned what it takes to be a legend. However, your bar is going to need much more than that to be successful. It's going to need great leadership.

This just in.

Those same attributes that make you a legend behind the bar will also make you a great leader. Busting your ass and having everyone's back will ensure that the owners and the team don't want to lose you. Why would they? You're a shining example for others.

Contrary to certain beliefs, a bartender's career doesn't have to end after being chewed up and spit out by the industry that made them.

It's true what they say: every bartender knows when they've poured their last drink. But there's a better option for someone hanging up their tins in our business.

A leadership position. You *do not* have to go quietly into the night.

Especially if you've established yourself as a legend that's earned that status by Pouring with Heart.

MOVING UP INTO LEADERSHIP POSITIONS

Though comparable in mindset and philosophy, leadership does come with a few different strokes than bartending. In leadership, you are guiding your team toward building regulars for the bar, instead of directly doing so yourself. It requires a broader view of, and focus on, what's best for growing your team and elevating the bar as a whole.

LEAD BARTENDER, BAR MANAGER, OR ASSISTANT GENERAL MANAGER

The next position above bartender is usually referred to as lead bartender. Lead bartenders take on nightly leadership behind the bar and often closeout duties as well. They can earn better tips since they get the best shifts, though it comes with a bit more responsibility. Lead bartenders spend a great deal of time in the crow's nest of their bar each night, overlooking their team as they navigate through their shift.

Bar managers and assistant general managers (AGM) are often depicted as similar roles. They're damn near interchangeable at most bars. Regardless of the decided-upon title, these positions tend to carry the second most responsibility in bars, essentially acting as the understudy for the GM position.

The lead bartender, bar manager, and assistant general manager positions make up our bar leadership teams. Which is why these positions require more than just Pouring with Heart with guests. They require doing so with everyone on the bar team. One of the main aspects to becoming a successful leader behind the bar is being fully of service to your team and building their trust. That's how you earn their respect and eventually earn further promotions down the line.

The first thing you need to know to graduate beyond the role of bartender is to articulate to the current general manager that you are committed to the bar long-term and want to be considered for a leadership position.

PAY ATTENTION: communicating your loyalty to the bar goes a long way. But truly understanding the requirements of that bar, and your potential leadership position, will lay out the yellow brick road to your promotion.

As a legendary bartender, you've made yourself indispensable in your bar. You'll be sure to have the ear of your general manager.

Use it.

The GM will be excited to have a legend like you teaching the rest of the bar team how to Pour with Heart.

And if they're smart, they'll pay you well for it too.

Once you've settled into your entry-level leadership position, your job is to bring out the best in your team. Many bartenders have personal insecurities holding them back, and they need encouragement to get over these in order to feel more confident talking to guests.

You remember what that was like, day one.

You can relate to your bar team in a way no one else can. Identifying with your staff, the same way you've practiced with endless guests, is a surefire way of building trust. A staff that believes in their leader tends to exhibit an easier time believing in themselves. In growing the kind of confidence it takes to make guests feel comfortable they made the right choice by going to your bar that night. Because they share a similar enthusiasm for your direction. Your passion.

The tremendous heart you've always poured with—*now*—you're paying forward.

Leading from the heart is so much more effective than leading with an iron fist.

Condescending leaders do not inspire the kind of loyalty necessary for growth.

They inspire turnover.

Ultimately, injecting confidence in those around you does wonders for your team. It also helps you stand out as a prime candidate to run *the entire bar*. To take on a task like that, you're going to want to have the whole staff (and ownership) behind you when the opportunity comes along.

GENERAL MANAGER (GM)

The top position at any bar is the general manager. One thing to know about your GM: no matter who it is, they always need help.

Every day, every hour, every fifteen minutes opens another Pandora's box for potential disaster. Equipment breaking down. Plumbing. Electrical. Sound system. Alarm system. Payroll system. Ordinances. Inventory. Drama on the staff that requires immediate attention.

Ask what responsibilities you can take off their plate.

Just please don't jump the gun and ask for more pay for doing these tasks. Look at it as a free education. If you can help with inventory, payroll, and ordering product, for example, you've just been comped a free course on learning the ropes to the business side of the bar. Not to mention that it shows proof of your dedication to taking on greater responsibilities.

As a GM, you must have the ability to solve the bar's problems.

That means you have to grow your skills as a critical thinker. We all have the capacity. It's really just a perspective shift. It takes focus and practice, but once you make the shift, you'll start seeing everything in a different light.

Where most people see problems, you'll visualize solutions.

You can start this process by picturing ways to solve your bar's problems ahead of time. Some answers are obvious, and some will require research. We have already discussed every bar's biggest problem: *how to build regulars*. So, by reading this book and becoming a legend behind the bar, you already know how to solve that problem.

Additionally, your time and expertise as a bartender has left you with intimate knowledge of the inefficiencies of the bar and how it can be improved. So start taking ownership in that and pride in bringing solutions to your GM.

After all, *you're the expert.*

Through brainstorming sessions with your GM, you'll begin to expand that expertise. Your general manager will certainly appreciate your support and solution-oriented approach.

Taking shit off their plate makes them look good.

By helping solve the bar's biggest problems and driving more regulars, your GM and eventually the owners will begin relying on you more and more each day.

Effective problem solving is the fastest way to build confidence among your bar team. The more fires you put out, the more they can focus on being completely of service and Pouring with Heart.

Alternatively, a bar staff that lacks confidence in their leaders' ability to tackle issues has a more difficult time getting through their shift, weighed down by the anxiety of what might happen when the next catastrophe pops up.

You know from experience how impossible it is to connect with your guest when the roof is caving in around you.

When you have confidence that your leader is going to bang out any problem under the sun, the bar staff feels like they're skating. That they're unstoppable. That their service has no restrictions and zero surprises looming over it.

Having that potential makes your staff feel invincible.

Bars are in constant need of another great leader. And GMs aren't exempt from the typically high turnover ratio of the industry. So, don't *get ready*.

Stay ready.

In our bar family, we exclusively promote from within because only then can we witness how a candidate really treats others. And how they solve problems. Leading is a big responsibility, and we want to hire and promote those who are conscientious and unselfish enough to put the staff and the bar's interests ahead of their own.

SHORTCUTS TO GETTING PROMOTED

There are none.

And if you find yourself in front of one, chances are it's a huge red flag. Your first indicator that you're actually doing something that is *NOT* grounds for getting promoted.

Like backstabbing, lying, or fucking over someone on your team. It's easy to do, which means you have to lean on your character in moments like these to spot it before you make a mistake you can't take back. Shortcuts, especially if they wind up veering down a malicious path, are transparent as hell and can stain the most stalwart reputation.

Don't pull that shit. Don't fuck over your family.

It's almost impossible to earn back their trust after you betray them.

Good leadership is about bringing people UP. So, if you're bringing people DOWN, it stands out like puke in a punchbowl. We all know someone with a shitty authority complex.

It reeks.

The responsibility of a good leader is to support their team. To elevate their team every step of the way. And like everything else in the bar world, it all begins with a choice.

Ask yourself, are you a rising tide that floats all ships?

Or are you sinking them?

Take care of everyone in your bar family, and have their fucking back. I promise they'll return the favor tenfold.

REFLECTIONS FROM PROVEN GENERAL MANAGERS
The following people are some of the most celebrated GMs in our bar family. These are their stories. How they came to earn leadership positions in the careers they love and show-case support for their bar teams at the highest level.

BART WALSH, GM OF LAS PERLAS MEZCAL BAR, LOS ANGELES

I was previously selling skincare, going from Costco to Costco, and I had a nervous breakdown because I hated that job. In

2016, I started barbacking [at Las Perlas], and I think it's good to start as a barback so by the time you get to GM, you know what it takes for the new people coming in, because you've been there. You still need to think like a barback, because you have to know every job as a GM.

The key to success in hospitality is you must have a genuine love of communication and making bonds with people, whether it's your staff, your superiors, other people in the industry, or most importantly, your guests. For me, I found a love that I didn't know I had. I didn't know that I loved hospitality so much. I discovered that through the bar business, and it is a genuine satisfaction—a genuine happiness that I get from connecting with guests, and now as GM, connecting with my staff. It's like I discovered a passion in life that I never knew I had.

STEPHANIE AGUILAR, GM OF SINGLE SPIRIT BARS, AUSTIN

I double-majored in French and theater. I didn't know what I wanted to do. Through a series of both unfortunate and very fortunate events, I was able to find the bar and the community. I love strangers. I often wander downtown alone because I like being able to walk into a bar or restaurant and just meet people. So yeah, that's kind of how I got into the hospitality industry. I don't see myself getting out of it. I just love the lifestyle too much.

To be a manager, you must have extreme empathy and intuition about people, and I've always been a very empathetic person. Since day one, I can see right through people, and I think that's why I like the bar business. There's something about working together on one team, one dream. It's essential for me. I enjoy teamwork.

I think I've grown in the industry because there were incredible people supporting me and a lot of opportunities. Like I said, it wasn't a box of false promises. It was more like this: if you really put your mind to it and you take the hospitality industry as it is, then you can create a personalized version of your hospitality and make that marketable.

CARRIE HELLER, GM OF THE NORMANDIE CLUB, LOS ANGELES

Every year, I wanted to do something different, and nothing really stuck until the bar business. I got my first foot into The Normandie Club in 2015. I started as a server, and that's what got me excited about finally feeling like this could be something to do with my whole life.

At that point, I didn't know that as a GM you could make a salary and get other benefits. I just thought, well, this is fun, and this can pay my bills for the time being, but I think it was the first time that I felt excited about what the future held.

When you work at a bar, I think it's a lot more exciting than just clocking in and clocking out. I think all of us, to an extent, want to be taken care of, and if you get a bunch of people together that all just want to take care of each other, you're naturally in this nice little cocoon of love. That's pretty indicative of the industry in general, and that's what enticed me to stay in it.

What has kept me on the management side of things is creating opportunities for others who aren't really sure what their path is. I love helping others find themselves, and that may mean they find a lifelong career in the bar world.

VICTOR DELGADO, GM OF SEVEN GRAND WHISKEY BAR, LOS ANGELES

I was going to college and also working as a behavioral therapist dealing with autistic children, which didn't support me financially. I was living with my parents. Then in 2009, I ended up jumping on the opportunity to be a barback at Seven Grand, and I was going home with more money than both my parents combined. I think I was twenty-six at the time, and since then, I never turned back. I've been with Seven Grand now for over eleven years. Not an ounce of regret for how I landed where I'm at now.

It's embedded in me to always serve others. So, to me, there's no better person to be serving you than a bartender. When opportunities presented themselves as an assistant general manager or as a GM, I always jumped on them. That's always been my nature. So, on a personal level, I've always thought, What's the next step and where am I going next? And, I just really love serving people. I also love hosting a party.

The bar business has made me more career-oriented, for sure, and it's made me take things a bit more seriously because I think in the past when I first started bartending, it was all about going out to bars and getting smashed. So, I think as you grow in the business and also as an individual, you have a choice. If you want to be a GM, you have to be a responsible person. So, I made the choice of always moving up and I had to stop fucking off. Your staff will always tell you when you're fucking up. They're not shy about letting you know.

REBECCA "BECKS" BIERBRAUER, GM OF SEVEN GRAND WHISKEY BAR, DENVER

When I was hired, I was very candid, almost too candid, and they gave me the job on the spot. What's interesting was that I found out after they hired me, on the first day of training, that I was pregnant with my second child.

I'm running into training, and I tell the GM...and he gives me a huge hug. The staff was so happy for me, they said they'd make it work, and they even bought me a pregnancy black apron so it would grow with me. They allowed me to be a pregnant working mother behind the bar, and they never gave me any flack about it.

They had my back, and I carried my daughter to term working behind the bar the entire time. They believed in me and just allowed my work ethic and my competency and everything else to shine through.

Soon, I took over all of the facets of actually running the bar, and then when the position above me opened up, it was just the natural next step. You have to just show up every day and be as good as you can be, every day. That's how I moved up the ranks from bartender to AGM to GM.

Some people think work in this industry is not for the long term. That it's just a part-time job. But this can be a career if it's done right and you treat your people well.

CHAPTER NINE

*DISCLAIMER TWO THE PITFALLS OF THE BAR BUSINESS

The bar business is a blast.

Music from the jukebox jamming to your favorite playlist. Loyal regulars shouting out your name when they walk in the door. Amorous singles giving you the eye.

Climbing the ladder to reach that top-shelf gem of a bottle shipped from the other side of the world. A healthy, thirsty line building up in front of your station with tips and praise alike to shower you with.

Makes you feel like you're on top of the world.

It's intoxicating. But like most intoxications, too much fun can be hazardous to your health.

Some nights you're invincible.

Other nights, you're barely holding on.

There's a power that comes along with being a bartender.

Being a rock star is a rush.

But that rock star life can take its toll. Fast.

Sure, the upside is awesome. Rock stars make gold records.
They sell out amphitheaters. They get laid.

A lot.

And they bring a ton of juice to the crowds they entertain.

But they also end up in rehab.

Or dead.

And by the time the party comes to a crashing halt, they've
hurt a lot of people.

When you're a big shot in this business…

The money is more than you've ever made in your life…

You're young, dumb, and full of rum…

You attract the pick of the litter each night…

And you find yourself with a little more time and access to party favors...

The chance of falling off the tightrope isn't just a concern. It's constantly in question.

Especially when it feels like there's great peril below your balancing act. Your footing wobbly while you bounce between stations behind the bar, hopscotching over a pit of vipers ready to strike.

Problem is, a lot of us get good at the *tiptoe*. Escaping the dangers of the snake pits and crocodile piles underneath.

It's easy to think you can do a line here and there, get drunk at work, bang someone on staff you shouldn't have, and get away with it. You do this again, you start to think you'll always get away with it.

Until you don't.

Maybe this chapter will be a waste of your time.

Maybe it will save your life.

Honestly, in this business, it could go either way.

I've witnessed several brilliant bar industry colleagues die in the prime of their lives on account of the health hazards related to our business. A close personal friend who was only thirty-eight when his heart gave out after living like a rock star for more than a decade. He was someone all of us looked up to, so it still chokes me up to think of him.

The hazards include alcohol and drug abuse, alcoholism, alcohol-related diseases, depression, mental illness, abysmal nutrition, peer pressure, and sleep deprivation.

In fact, based on statistical death rates, bartending is considered more dangerous than first-line firefighting supervisors—whose most common cause of death is listed as fires and explosions.

I've learned a ton from other industry professionals the hard way. And with your permission, I'd like to share my insight on some recurring dangers you could find yourself exposed to in the bar industry. It's my hope that this chapter will illuminate how you can avoid being another industry death statistic.

Because the hazards can take any of us if we let them.

I'm not trying to kill the good times. Harsh your mellow or check your vibe. But there's a time to ride the dragon. And then there's a time to make smart decisions.

I'm on your side.

This chapter is not about judgment.

It's about recognition.

NINE LIVES

I remember my first bar, The Liquid Kitty. We raged. Every night turned into after hours. Pretty soon, it was hard to tell when the party stopped and the next one began. I was barely sleeping. Chain-smoking. Drugs everywhere. Booze coming out of my pores.

Just a mess.

What I wasn't aware of at the time was that the never-ending debauchery put me at an incredible risk to blow it all. Not just everything I'd built up to that point. But the twenty-five-year career I've been blessed with ever since.

My two beautiful kids.

All of it—could have been gone.

With one untimely bad decision in the eye of one of those hurricane benders.

Not only that, but when I think of the future careers and lives that would have been impacted by me screwing up something special for others before it even started, it makes me take inventory.

How close I might have come to jeopardizing everything because I wasn't looking at the bigger picture.

The idea of losing out on the opportunity to create careers—my calling in life—because of poor choices I could have easily avoided makes me want to puke.

What the nonstop party was, was a parade of disillusion.

It's a blur for a reason.

The "party" doesn't want you to recognize the lows. When you step back and take a sober look, believe me, *they're there.*

And they stick with you a lot longer than any of the highs.

The thing is, it happens to us all.

The hardworking. The talented. The committed. The educated. The earnest. The careful and even the conservative. It only takes one time to shoot yourself in the foot.

The hazards don't discriminate. They do not care who they take down. What relationships they ruin. Who's health and safety they put at risk.

And when they get their hooks in you, *they anchor.*

Which means when you're dabbling in the fray, it's hard to get off the ride.

The scary part is that once we're on the ride long enough, we start to develop an invincibility complex.

We normalize a bump. Then a line. Then an eight ball.

A joint. Then an eighth. Then a pound.

We drink to be social.

Then we drink enough to kill a horse.

The truth hurts. I know. But we're in this together.

We're family.

I don't want you to end up dead. The truth is, we don't have nine lives.

I've seen enough fucking tragedy. And though the pain from those I've lost is only a fraction of their family's hurt, it *never* gets any easier hearing bad news.

FRIENDS IN LOW PLACES

Often, when we're hammered, it looks like we're surrounded by friends. That's usually true when you and your crew get together for a night out on the town. A barbecue. The beach. Mardi Gras. A kick-back in your parent's home with your neighborhood buds.

But then there's the times we're fucked up after a shift. It's four a.m. and we're in a dangerous place with seedy, untrustworthy people—*not friends*—that are likely in that spot for the same ill reasons you found yourself there.

Eventually the carousel of rock 'n' roll stops. If you wake up from a bad dream next to users, pushers, indulgers, well... everything has a price.

They may be there with you. But if any kind of shit goes down, they won't be there *for you*.

Being mindful starts with the company you keep.

ACCESSIBILITY AND PEER PRESSURE IN BARS

While alcohol may be the most widely available poison for the picking, you can bet your ass it's not the ONLY thing waiting in the wings.

Different streaks for different freaks. Each more dangerous than the next without a little self-control and the solid support of your bar family around you.

All the more reason why we've got to have each other's back. Why we can't burn the faith and trust we've worked so hard to earn from our bar team.

Tim Etherington-Judge is the head of Healthy Hospo, an international charitable organization committed to helping people in the bar industry. To Tim, one of the hidden dangers of this business is "the peer pressure to always go harder, to have that extra shot. We encourage too much bad behavior, and we also bully people if they don't want to take part in it."

It's so true.

I remember being in one of my bars and overhearing a bartender explain to another bartender on shift that they were taking it easy from booze and not drinking. In response, the other bartender took it upon himself to laugh and called him "a pussy."

Perhaps he thought he was being playful.

Maybe in his mind, that was true. But in truth, his behavior wasn't playful. It was toxic.

And dangerous.

It was *anything but* Pouring with Heart.

Peer pressure sends the complete opposite message of our shared values, while selfishly projecting one's own agenda over that of the person you're supposed to be in complete service to.

And as for the person's safety on the losing end of that toxicity? Devil may care.

On the other hand, we all have a personal responsibility to stand on our own two feet when being propositioned. Egged on. Fucked with.

For those of you who already know this, great. It's still worth reiterating.

Here's the deal. You don't have to drink when you don't want to drink. Some bartenders get this confused. They figure they *honor* and respect alcohol. Sell it all day and all night. Dedicate their lives to making drinks for the delight of their guests and our industry.

Seems almost heresy to deny a drink. A shot. A cocktail offered your way.

Hear me when I say, *clearly*, that none of that shit is related to one another.

You have nothing to prove to anybody, or our industry, if you're being pressured for not having another drink. We all have a different tolerance for alcohol. Being in a pissing contest based on who can do more shots is a loser's game. You won't become a badass in this business by outdrinking anybody.

You'll just have more hangovers.

And more days full of espresso, greasy food, dark sunglasses... and apology lists.

ALCOHOLISM AND BARTENDING

Access to so much alcohol in the bar industry is obviously a big issue, particularly if you are an alcoholic. If you are, look to work for an employer who will support you in your sobriety.

Regardless, the right bar for anyone shouldn't pressure its employees to drink alcohol. In my experience, alcoholism is something real and respected by those who are sober and taking the steps to stay that way. I revere, and support, some legendary bartenders and bar owners who stay entirely "off the sauce."

Alcoholism is an ensnaring damn disease. For alcoholics, one drink often leads to *dozens* more. If that's you, get help before it swallows up your career. Good leaders will recognize this, if you're honest with them. The right bar will empathize and empower you to be successful without having to compromise.

I advocate Alcoholics Anonymous (AA) and their abundant meetings, open to everyone in every city.

DRUGS AREN'T HARD TO FIND

Drugs are available at every bar, if you know where to look.

But once you start using certain drugs while trying to work—particularly cocaine—it's insanely difficult to stop.

It's an insidious drug that inflates your ego at every turn. That turn may feel like a good idea in the short term. And if that's what you're chasing, off the clock, in a safe place for you and others—have a ball. Who am I to judge what you do in your personal life?

However, if you're doing it *on the clock*, and you're interested in maximizing your chances for success in that bar and becoming a legendary bartender, the devil's dandruff can take your career aspirations and drop them off a fucking cliff.

Especially if you find yourself adhering to the illusion that doing lines is the best way to counteract how drunk you might be. Yes, uppers and downers balance one another, but it's a fallacy to say an equal amount of both regulates you.

Here's an equation for you.

Fucked up on booze + fucked up on coke DOES NOT = being sober.

FOOD AND SLEEP

Being healthy in this business means more than just not over-drinking over overdrugging. It also means not overdoing it on bad food. Nutrition is a direct line to your health. Good or bad, we are what we eat.

Bartenders often eat fast food when on their breaks and, even more so, after their shift. Late-night junk food leads to potential obesity (from going to bed with a brick full of grease and carbs in your belly) and the rabbit hole of health problems that come with that. Instead of fast food, try eating a healthy, home-cooked meal before your shift. This will give you more natural, sustainable energy and help protect you from giving into less healthy temptations later.

Sleep deprivation is so common in the bar business, it's really more like the norm. And it's much more dangerous than people realize. According to Etherington-Judge, "a growing number of scientists think that sleep deprivation may be the world's leading cause of death."

Because of distractions like smartphones, video games, and social media, people today are getting much less sleep than they should. Bartenders are particularly at risk because of the nocturnal nature of their shifts.

Where the average person is working their nine to five, the bartender is often logging the five to nine—p.m. to a.m.

Often, we have that vampire schedule that sees the sun rise before we go to bed. Nothing like showing up to a restaurant for dinner after your shift, and finding only the breakfast menu available.

Etherington-Judge found that "hospitality is one of the most sleep-deprived industries in the world, and lack of sleep can exacerbate your chances of having a heart attack, cancer, and all sorts of other diseases, and it really has a big impact on your mental health."

DEPRESSION (AND OTHER MENTAL ILLNESSES)

Depression and mental illness are big issues in every industry.

Etherington-Judge cites that 20 percent of people under forty suffer from some form of mental health problem.

In the hospitality industry, that statistic leaps to 33 percent.

Which means the next time you're in a room of ten people and you feel like you're suffering unlike anyone else, remember that shared hurt is more common than you think.

Resources *feel* more available to you when you realize you're not the only one.

You can/should get help. An excellent resource available to you is Healthy Hospo. Also check out Restaurant Recovery, and of course, don't hesitate to reach out to a mental illness specialist in your area.

If you suspect you might need help, even in the least. Get help.

Statistics show depression to be highly correlated to not having enough love, compassion, and purpose in our lives. It stems from a major lack of serotonin and oxytocin.

Pouring with Heart combats this.

But if you're feeling low and you're not up to Pouring with Heart at the moment, my best advice is to go be around others *that are*. It will feed your own heart and soul with positive chemicals that feel rewarding, boost confidence, and can be a ladder for you up and out from the pitfalls of depression.

A lot of people suffering from a lack of serotonin and oxytocin don't have the reset button you do. That new guest standing in front of your well. Every time someone walks in the door, there is a new, fresh opportunity for you to get that healthy high.

Likely, it's a person who might need you just as much as you need them.

CONCLUSION

"And now here is my secret, a very simple secret:
It is only with the heart that one can see rightly;
what is essential is invisible to the eye."
−Antoine de Saint-Exupéry, The Little Prince

In this book, you've been introduced to the heart's lens. And how looking through its lens lends you the secret to building a career in this business, the right way.

Without heart, a bartender resembles a robot. No soul. No life. No *veritas*.

An inability to empathize. Sympathize. *Feel* for their guests and their team.

The heart has the power to bring humanity together. To build relationships and bonds invisible to the naked eye.

It's why aesthetics, by themselves, don't mean shit. They're *cool*. But they won't bring anybody back without having soul in their foundation. Without heart.

People will forget about the disco ball chandelier on the ceiling, the stag heads mounted on the wall, and the two-thousand-pound bar top made of Santos mahogany.

And they'll forget about you too.

But when you tap into the unbridled power of your heart and are completely of service, not only will they remember you.

They'll remember you as a legend.

It's the heartbeat of a bar that builds regulars. Beating that drum is YOU.

The bartender we love.

Sometimes the romance of it all gives me pause.

In the cocktail of life, bartenders aren't the rocks. The spirit. Or the fancy fresh ingredients.

They're the glass.

Holding it all together for us while we mix, stir, and shake our way through this batshit crazy thing we call life.

The more heart, the more LOVE that glass supports.

Be the glass.

Now, there is no cheat sheet for Pouring with Heart.

So, if you were looking for a quick buck or a quick answer on how to build a career in the bar business, sorry, friend.

You bought the wrong book.

It takes work. And it takes time. But I promise it'll be more than worth it.

It's a tough fucking world out there, and there is more noise and distraction every day.

Without support from the relationships we make with loved ones, we're fucked.

Pouring with Heart offers us the chance to make a profound impact on those we're closest to. Best friends. Partners. Parents. Children. Unselfishly taking care of those around you helps enrich them all for the better. And your loved ones, *your family*, will admire you for it.

Included in that can be your *new* bar family and the regulars who come into your bar.

After all, they're the ones who will feel and feed off the serotonin you're creating night in and night out. Soon, the most orphaned of us all ends up with family coming out of their ears.

I've seen, and moreover, *felt* how Pouring with Heart has transformed people in an incredible way.

You've borne witness to it in the interviews I've included in this book. If *their* lives were transformed for the better…and *mine* was transformed for the better…goddamn, I can't wait to learn what it does for *you*.

I've been fortunate enough to help create the careers of close to four hundred amazing folks in this industry, and I promise to dedicate the rest of my life to creating many, many more.

Any bar has the ability to turn a derelict neighborhood into a thriving community. It's been true throughout the history of this country. And that history only repeats itself.

We, as an industry, can make a tremendous impact by Pouring with Heart together.

The more love, the more community, the better.

In a world growing more heartless by the day, it's time for our industry to enlarge our heart. To remind ourselves that we are the place people choose to connect and celebrate humanity.

The place we all can go to break out of our shells and expand our horizons. Treat everyone as our brothers and sisters. And be appreciated for *exactly who we are*.

In this industry, taking care of each other is our direct responsibility. To set a good example for others to follow.

The legend Gary Regan said toward the end of his remarkable life that he thought bartenders could change the world. That may sound grandiose.

Until you read his quote:

It's your job to be of service to your guest, so that when she leaves your bar, she's happier than when she walked in. If you achieve that, then you are changing the world. That guest will pass that happiness along to the very next person she meets, and it will get paid forward over and over again.

Regan's right.

One good deed begets another. The same way negativity and cancers of the world spread, so does the light.

He continued:

Suppose you make ten people feel great on a Friday night. And then those ten people pay it forward to another ten people? Now, suppose that fifty bartenders in your town did the same thing. And that fifty bartenders in fifty thousand towns and cities each made ten people happy on that same Friday night.

That's 25 million new smiles out there by the weekend.

The human heart, with its immense capacity to love and be loved, can be the central driving force in eradicating isolation, loneliness, and disconnection.

Which means Pouring with Heart can change the world.

Bartenders…can change the world.

YOU. Can change the world.

Muhammad Ali, the greatest fighter of all time, said, "Service to others is the rent you pay for your room here on earth."

He got it.

And he changed the world.

So much so that he's remembered more for his healing than his fighting. His humanitarianism. Because again, like Maya Angelou told us, people don't remember what you did. They remember how you made them feel.

For bartenders, *that's all* you do.

But it's still something that you *have to do*. It doesn't happen by itself.

You have to get off your ass and go get it.

Build regulars. Build a career. Build your legacy.

And Pour with motherfucking Heart.

APPENDIX

RECOMMENDED COCKTAIL BOOKS

The Art of the Bar: Cocktails Inspired by the Classics, Jeff Hollinger

Cocktail Codex: Fundamentals, Formulas, Evolutions, Alex Day, David Kaplan, and Nick Fauchald

CO Specs: Recipes & Histories of Classic Cocktails, Cas Oh

The Dead Rabbit Grocery and Grog Drinks Manual: Secret Recipes and Barroom Tales from Two Belfast Boys Who Conquered the Cocktail World, Sean Muldoon, Jack McGarry, and Ben Schaffer

Death & Co: Modern Classic Cocktails, Alex Day, David Kaplan, and Nick Fauchald

Drinking Distilled: A User's Manual, Jeffrey Morgenthaler

Drinking Like Ladies: 75 Modern Cocktails from the World's Leading Female Bartenders, Kirsten Amann and Misty Kalkofen

Harry Johnson's Bartender Manual, Harry Johnson

Imbibe!: From Absinthe Cocktail to Whiskey Smash, a Salute in Stories and Drinks to "Professor" Jerry Thomas, Pioneer of the American Bar, Updated and Revised Edition, David Wondrich

The Joy of Mixology, Revised and Updated Edition, Gary Regan

Meehan's Bartender Manual, Jim Meehan

The New Craft of the Cocktail, Revised and Updated Version, Dale DeGroff

Punch: The Delights (and Dangers) of the Flowing Bowl, David Wondrich

Regarding Cocktails, Sasha Petraske and Georgette Moger-Petraske

Spirits of Latin America: A Celebration of Culture & Cocktails, with 100 Recipes from Leyenda & Beyond, Ivy Mix

The Ultimate Bar Book: The Comprehensive Guide to Over 1,000 Cocktails, Mittie Hellmich

Unvarnished: A Gimlet-Eyed Look at Life Behind the Bar, Eric Alperin and Deborah Stoll

ACKNOWLEDGMENTS

This book wouldn't have been possible for me to write without the help of so many people.

The biggest contributor was my co-writer Erik Cardona, who, thanks to his experience writing professionally and Pouring with Heart for years as a bartender in our bar family, helped me share my truth. Thanks, brother!

I must also thank those who contributed directly to the book. I appreciate the thoughtful input from my executive leadership team—Andrew Abrahamson, Peter Stanislaus, and Eric Needleman—which made this book so much better at every turn. As well as the interviews with Eric Alperin, Pedro Shanahan, Ivy Mix, Steve Robbins, Carrie Heller, Miguel Alonso, Stephanie Aguilar, Bart Walsh, Victor Delgado, Becks Bierbrauer, and Tim Etherton-Judge.

I want to thank my coach David Daugherty for pushing me to write this book and continuing to give feedback along the way. No matter how long it took. Along with my professional coaches Jason Rush, Taylor Brown, and Sean Finter for always being there for our bar group.

And I really appreciate everyone at Scribe for motivating me and giving me a framework to put this book together. Thank you Sarafina Riskind and Bailey Hayes for being my publishing managers and keeping me on task. A special thanks to Tucker Max for inspiring me early on. Your personal note regarding the book's message gave me a lot of fire throughout the writing process. And lastly, thanks to my editors Paul Fair and Hal Clifford for relating so much to the material and helping me improve it.

I want to thank my close friends Arya, Marc, Robert, Liana, and Vidal for giving me tremendous encouragement along the way. And I'd like to recognize Matt Webb, David Childs, Christian Kneedler, Marc Smith, and Ricki Kline for supporting and encouraging me to go into the bar business in the first place.

This book wouldn't exist, nor would our bar group, without the support of my partners and investors over the last twenty-five years. I want to thank you all for believing in our crazy dream of creating 2030 careers by 2030. Especially Mark and Lani Verge, Steve and Jaime Gumins, Aroon Chinai, Pamela Moses, Eric and Megan Needleman, and the Weiss Family.

Thank you, Dale "King Cocktail" DeGroff, for writing the foreword to this book. I've always looked up to you. And to Cameron Scott and Noel Carlon, who Poured with Heart and made a permanent positive impact on our bar family, these pages are in your memory.

Lastly, I couldn't write this book without the loving support of my amazing kids, Maxwell and Violette. My beautiful mother, who has always pushed me to follow strong values. And in tribute to my father, Ed, who inspired me to follow my passion in life. He would say, "Otherwise you are full of shit and Shinola."

This book and our success wouldn't exist without all the great people who make up the entire Pouring With Heart Family.

ABOUT THE AUTHORS

CEDD MOSES

Cedd Moses is the Founder and Chief Vision Officer of Pouring With Heart, a hospitality company that operates twenty-five bars, historic restaurants, and beer halls across Los Angeles, San Diego, Austin, and Denver.

Moses and his team of pioneers garnered national recognition for their part in revitalizing Downtown LA circa 2002. Today, you can find their bars growing across the country, with Moses also spearheading the For Each Other Fund, a charity that supports Pouring With Heart bar staff in need.

All profits of this book will go to the For Each Other Fund.

ERIK CARDONA

Erik Cardona is an author, screenwriter, lyricist, columnist, copywriter, and two-time festival winner with awards from both Bentonville and the LA Film Festival.

Before beginning his writing career, Cardona could be found Pouring with Heart, bartending at the legendary Seven Grand Whiskey Bar in LA, where he shared in the creation and development of Bar Jackalope, voted Best Whiskey Bar in Los Angeles by *LA Weekly Magazine* in 2014.

Made in the USA
Las Vegas, NV
14 December 2021

37635582R00163